HERTFORDSHIRE

A Shell Guide

Great Amwell

>   . . . How beautiful,
> How various is yon view! delicious hills
> Bounding smooth vales, smooth vales by winding streams
> Divided, that here glide thro' grassy banks
> In open sun, there wander under shade
> Of aspen tall, or ancient elm, whose boughs
> O'erhang grey castles, and romantic farms . . .

John Scott (1730–83)
Amwell

A Shell Guide

HERTFORDSHIRE

by R.M. Healey

Faber and Faber   3 Queen Square   London

First published in 1982
by Faber and Faber Limited
3 Queen Square London WC1N 3AU
Printed in Great Britain by
Fakenham Press Limited
Fakenham, Norfolk
All rights reserved

Lamppost museum, **Great Amwell**

British Library Cataloguing in Publication Data

Healey, R.M.
  A Shell guide to Hertfordshire.
  1. Hertfordshire—Description and travel—
  Guide-books
  I. Title
  914.25′80458   DA670.H5

  ISBN 0–571–11801–1

St Albans, south arcade of nave ▷

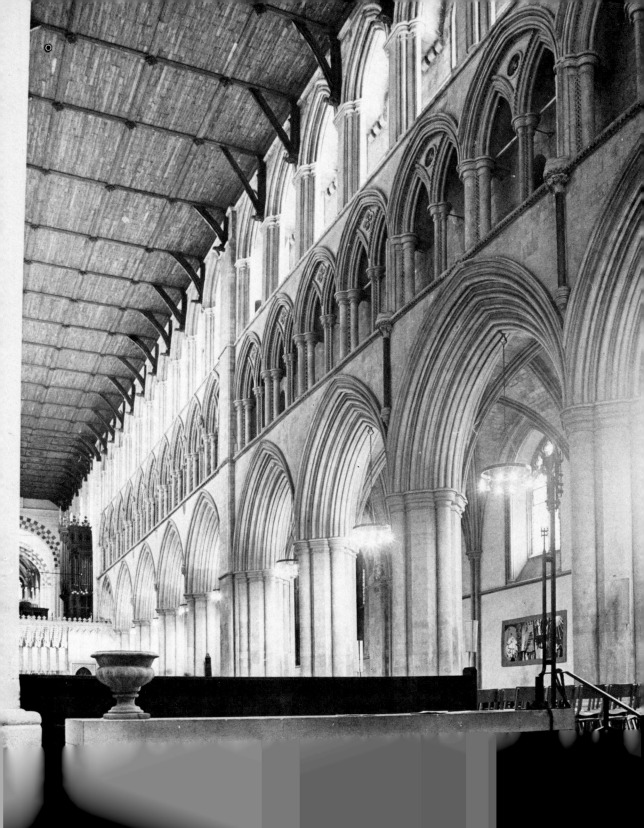

Acknowledgements

I would like to thank all those who have helped me in my research for this book—in particular those whom I have met on my travels around Hertfordshire, and others who have shown an interest in the project. I owe special thanks to Miss Patricia Huskinson for her all-round encouragement.

Although disagreeing with some of his opinions I owe much to Prof. Pevsner's pioneering work on English architecture. I should also like to thank John and Myfanwy Piper for their help and hospitality over the last six years.

Finally, I dedicate this book to my mother, whose patience, I hope, has at last been rewarded.

Barkway,
Herts.,
March,
1982.

Local character:
Diamond End,
Peter's Green (*above*);
Salisbury Hall,
Shenley (*below*)
Nuthampstead

Illustrations

Note: Captions to the photographs include place names in **bold type**. These refer to entries in the gazetteer, pages 39–187.

Berkhampsted castle and moat

Anstey castle and moat ▷

Introduction

The Landscape of Man

Mrs Munt in E. M. Forster's *Howards End* (1910) surveys the red roof-tops of Stevenage from its station and immediately feels the doubts and misgivings of many a newcomer to Hertfordshire. What lies beyond—England or suburbia? Forster affirms that England it is—though an Albion under threat from dehumanizing forces. He recognizes London in the 'residential estates'. More recently, expatriate poet Donald Davie, in a long-range recollection from Berkeley, California, saw cracked pave-ments in an 'Anglo-Jewish enclave between Finchley and Barnet' (Totteridge perhaps?) as a fit image of what the county had become. Both men were guilty of doing Hertfordshire an injustice.

More than neighbouring Essex and Buckinghamshire, much more than Berkshire and Kent, and even Surrey, Hertfordshire gets undervalued and sometimes dismissed by travel-writers and tourists. Nobody thinks of renting a Hertfordshire farmhouse for a holiday. Yet there are farms in open country at Bushey and Shenley—only 15 miles from

△ Westmill

▽ Benington

Anstey estate cottages (*above*)
Hertford Heath (*centre*) ▷
Tring (*below*)

Baldock (*above*); Hemel Hempstead (*below*)

Hunton Bridge △

Charing Cross. Horses graze happily in the fields by Metroland's Moor Park. A bare or wooded landscape beckons over every half-timbered gable of every suburban street—and never does the suburbia plummet to the banal depths of Thames-side Essex, or achieve the relentlessness of Greater Croydon, or the ordinariness of south Bucks. Certainly there are New Towns of brick boxes, new roads, lines of striding pylons, and subtopia; but the scale is small, rather intimate. For those prepared to approach the county unblinkered and unprejudiced it is a continual delight discovering just how much the depredations have spared.

First, here are the facts: though no longer one of England's smallest counties Hertfordshire, with around 1 million people occupying about 630 square miles, is still small and densely populated. It teems beside Lincolnshire or Shropshire, for instance. Yet Watford with only 77,000 people is the largest town, closely followed by Stevenage and Hemel Hempstead. After St Albans (56,000) comes Welwyn Garden City (47,000), and then Letchworth, Hitchin, Hatfield, Harpenden, Rickmansworth and Hoddesden hover around the 30,000 mark. Hertford, the county town and main administrative centre, has a mere 22,000 people, making it one of the smallest county towns in England.

(*above*) near **Peter's Green**   near **Sandridge** △

◁ (*centre*) **Ashwell**

(*below*) near **Hinxworth**   **Anstey** ▽

Ashwell

London overspill has swelled towns in the north and east, like Royston, Buntingford and Stortford—once strictly agricultural—and brought new industries to replace some of the dying ones. London commuters continue to be drawn towards these outlying districts as well as the more familiar territories farther south. Yet the growth of housing and industry is well controlled and entirely in keeping with Hertfordshire's character—which is essentially that of an agricultural county which happens to be close to London.

Hertfordshire has a straightforward topography. Its key geological elements of chalk, clay and flint are so dispersed that all the natural wonders craved by the tourist—beetling cliffs, craggy hillsides, wide plains, vast forests—can never occur. These types of feature arise in miniature, or have been tamed, licked into shape by Man through the ages. In vain we look for the 'wild Nature' loved by the Lake poets. Charles Lamb liked Hertfordshire because he felt safe in its lanes and fields and ancient well-bred homes. The hand of the farmer and the improver could be seen wherever he looked—in the fields, woodland, plantations, parkland and prosperous farmhouses—all components of a sort of informal Arcadia based on the principle that natural beauty is born of the prosperity and well-

Barkway

being brought about by Man's harnessing of Nature—and not of Nature untamed. Little has changed since Lamb's time. Hertfordshire's parkland and estates remain its pride, and are almost unchanged in character and extent; but the commons and woodland, if anything, are shrinking still further under the hand of the farmer—who remains the chief landscape architect. There are three main types of landscape.

In the north the great Bedfordshire/ Cambridgeshire plain laps at the foot of a long Chiltern spur that sweeps across from near Luton to Barley and beyond, and is basically chalk overlaid with heavy clay-with-flints. The resulting downland, best seen immediately south of Royston, and more especially between Barkway, Barley and Reed, is characterized by vast prairie fields of wheat and barley—the consequence of modern intensive farming doing away with the ancient hedges and coppices. It is a vision of beaten gold in summer, with fields tilting down to hidden chalk streams marked by columns of ash-trees, with here and there a disused chalk-pit catching the sun, and a dash of red indicating a lonely farm. Here Hertfordshire comes closest to the sublime—but it is Man's doing, not Nature's. Farther east, looking towards Essex, the roll-

ing fields are ironed out somewhat, and in well-wooded districts, like the Pelhams and around Much Hadham, pastoral scenes which recall Samuel Palmer's Kent supervene and are particularly exquisite. Corn seas wash up against ash plantations rank with dog's mercury; there are cavernous yew woods and sudden outcrops of hornbeam and beech. Hedges and ancient tracks tend to be retained. But there are no sheep on the uplands, and cattle are only to be seen in the river valleys. But in east Hertfordshire the rivers, with a few obvious exceptions, are hardly more than streams, and the chalk streams which feed them, as they eventually feed the Lea, are no more than trickles that dry up in the summer and leave ditches—as at Great Hormead and Aspenden. Yet these streams have helped to make north and east Hertfordshire one of the richest grain belts in southern England—and thereby made Leaside the centre of the English malting industry.

The Hertfordshire landscape most familiar to travellers going into or out of London by train is often disparaged. It was Mrs Munt's first view of the county—the terraces built on city clay gave way to the speculative estates of Barnet and then the sandy heathland of Potters Bar. After this

Near **Little Gaddesden**

the railway and Great North Road ran through gentle, unremarkable scenes of river and wide valley; of birch, bracken and willow; of parkland and golf-links, and neat red-brick villas on the outskirts of towns; and finally to Stevenage and beyond. But since those days, despite the coming of the Garden Cities and the New Towns, whose boundaries now encircle much woodland and many villas, little has changed in this most easily recognizable belt of Hertford-shire—and one might say the same of that similar and peculiarly evocative landscape between Watford and Colney Heath—and indeed of much of the county's unassuming scenery that has been generally misprized.

Undoubtedly Hertfordshire's biggest vis-ual assets are its hilly areas of wooded heath and its Chiltern woodland. Of the former, by far the greatest zone lies south and west of the Lea valley and acts as a vital buffer (despite urban interruptions at Cuffley and Goffs Oak) between burgeoning Enfield and Hertford. Over much of the underlying clay are gravel and sand, giving rise to the light oak woodlands and fir plantations, which around Bayford and Little Berkhamsted, for instance, recall parts of the Ashdown and

(*above*) near **Hexton**; (*below*) **Berkhampsted** Common ▷

Near **Barley**

Wyre forests. In total contrast the magnificent beechwoods that adorn most of south Buckinghamshire appear only to thrive in certain corners of the Hertfordshire Chilterns—generally from Great Gaddesden to the county boundary south of Tring, and most spectacularly in Ashridge Park (National Trust). Yet West Hertfordshire, though dominated by chalk, does not (by virtue, for instance, of its many rivers) present the simple geology of the east—which is why a careful tour of a typical district—around Sarratt, say, with all its surprises and diversities—can be such an

exquisite experience. Possibly one's oddest encounter in Hertfordshire is with the Wirral-shaped peninsula of chalky clay that pokes into the Aylesbury plain from the Chilterns at Tring. Surveying the level landscape at Puttenham it is hard to believe that Barkway is in the same county.

Hertfordshire has a flora strongly influenced by the predominant chalk. When outcrops push through heavy clays there are the familiar reds, yellows, and blues in the coarse grass, or battening on to the flint-pitted chalk itself, flowers that are known, loved, and too often despised all over

Near Puttenham

southern England—the poppies, celandines, campions, violets of the hedgerow and wayside. One of the most memorable sights of the early summer in the prairie uplands of the north and east is of the poppies invading the fields of greenish-gold like a bright rash, and then perhaps spilling over with white campion and cow-parsley to make fields of dual-carriageway verges. In the districts of pure clay-with-flints most chalk-loving plants remain, although there are fewer now than before due to the wholesale grubbing-up of hedges. The picture one takes away from a tour of the Essex border (Anstey or the Pelhams, say) is of clematis and bryony-clad straggly hawthorn hedges punctuated by lonely ash-trees, and plantations, generally of ash, too, which are so heavily overgrown with a suffocating carpet of dog's mercury that all soil fungi and all but half-a-dozen of the commonest wild flowers are excluded. Naturally fungi are discouraged by heavy clay, and in Hertfordshire will only usually appear on lawns, in leaf-litter (Chiltern beechwoods especially), in sandy-soiled woodlands (Moor Park, Northaw Great Wood, Broxbourne Woods) and in some damp ditches.

The Hertfordshire flora, though indeed unremarkable, includes one or two exotics —and a few rarities. The complex geology of the river valleys, particularly those in the highly urbanized south-west corner of the county, produces the poisonous thorn-apple, henbane and deadly nightshade—all equally lovers of chalk and waste places. Nightshade was once cultivated on a commercial scale near Hitchin. The poisonous green hellebore, a handsome plant and not common, likes stony places only, and close to Stevenage a whole wood glows with its pale fire. Rare orchids native to Hertfordshire include: bird's-nest, military, frog, bee; and the exceptionally scarce burnt, lizard and man. These are found mainly in the Chilterns, as is the Chiltern gentian, a plant that has only been traced to *one* spot in the county. Therfield Heath, near Royston, is the best-known home of the modest Pasque flower, which grows in numbers among the downland grass. But most spectacular of all in the calendar of exotica is the giant hogweed, a species whose habit of spreading makes it anathema to many, but whose presence in an otherwise featureless tract, as at Chapel Green, near Buckland, is a triumph.

Hertfordshire, unlike Wiltshire, is no cradle of British civilization. Like any other well-drained chalk county in southern England it has evidence of pre-history in its tumuli, its Iron Age hill forts and camps, its one or two Belgic settlements, and its mysterious Icknield Way. But these examples are few, and not really outstanding. Only the Icknield Way, as it scores through chalk on its determined route between Salisbury Plain and East Yorkshire, exercises the imagination. For how old is the 'Way'? Possibly it was a track made and used by neolithic man to transport the best flint tools from the Grime's Grave mines to central southern England. Since then parts of it in

Hertfordshire have become village lane, county boundary and even dual carriageway—as well as deep-rutted track through buckthorn bushes, as it is in the parishes of Lilley and Hexton, in the county's northern heights.

If the evocative Icknield Way is a tourist 'must', what the Romans left behind after their occupation can be appreciated in Ermine, Akeman and Watling streets, which must have served the occupiers well and are still (in many cases) used as roads. Two of them cross at Hertfordshire's primary Roman site of Verulamium, which was built by the water meadows below the present St Albans. Only comparatively recently in their history have enough of the flint and tile chunks and other remains been laid bare to prove the extent and magnificence of what was once Roman Britain's most important city.

The Saxons left indications of their building style in a few churches like Reed, Westmill and St Albans cathedral—but the bequest was minimal. Hertfordshire is not, unlike Northamptonshire, a fruitful hunting ground. Yet the enigmatic Grims Ditch (or Dyke), which winds its way through Chiltern woods and fields, was undoubtedly a very effective Saxon boundary ditch, and is still surprisingly deep in places. The wider and deeper trenches near Wheathampstead (Slad and Devil's Dyke) are more likely to be Iron Age or Belgic than Saxon.

Because Hertfordshire has no building stone all its medieval churches are of flint and mortar and have tracery and dressings either of clunch from Ashwell and Bedfordshire's Totternhoe, or from the quarries of Northamptonshire and Rutland. It is possible that some stone came from as far afield as the Cotswolds, via the Icknield Way. Certainly imported clunch can be found in churches near this ancient route. But this

Icknield Way,
near **Lilley** ▷

▽ Devil's Dyke,
Wheathampstead

Queen Hoo Hall, **Tewin**

clunch, an odd material half-way between chalk and stone, has been shown to be highly unsuitable. Look, for instance, at Ashwell's mighty church tower, or Hinxworth's leprous tracery, or Caldecote's soggy water stoup. But to see clunch used extensively as a building material one must certainly visit Ashwell village, and then cross the border into southern Bedfordshire.

(*above*) **Brent Pelham**; (*below*) **Hinxworth** Place ▷

Moats at Salisbury Hall, **Shenley** (*above*), and **Anstey** (*right*)

Therfield (*above*)
Ashwell (*below*)

Norton △
Ashwell ▽

△
▽ **Aldenham**

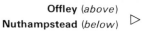**Offley** (*above*)
Nuthampstead (*below*) ▷

When Hertfordshire had much more woodland than it now has the timber-framed building was the natural outcome, and this style of the vernacular lasted at least until the late 17th century. Most of the towns and villages can boast a sample of medieval timbering, and some—like Hitchin, Hertford and St Albans—hint at much more than they show. Fifty years ago Watford's High Street was crammed with medieval buildings. Now only a handful remain. Hertfordshire's proximity to London has naturally put pressure on towns like Watford, but more significantly has exposed the practical vernacular architecture of this agricultural county to the building fads of the metropolis. As only the rich could afford fashionable brick it was usually the best timber-framed houses that were either razed or more often lost to posterity behind a smart brick casing. This has been the case in Tilehouse Street, Hitchin—but there are numerous instances throughout the county involving hall houses, manor-houses and others. Moreover the destruction has lately spread to timber-framed barns, of which there were, and still are, many handsome examples. Visit those at Caldecote before they too collapse and are replaced by the all too familiar Dutch type. But Hertfordshire, even if it had lost less, could never match the richness and variety of, say, Essex's timber-framing heritage. There is no Saffron Walden or Coggeshall, no Paycocke's House, though there are thousands of humbler black and white and plastered cottages left.

Generally one can say that Hertfordshire's neighbours have had their influence on the regional building styles: Essex, with her weather-boarding, plaster and thatch, in the east; Cambridgeshire, with her peculiar white and yellow brick, in the north; in the far west one could be anywhere in the Buckinghamshire Chilterns; and London, in the south, still exerts the most powerful influence of all. And today, brick appears to be the commonest material in every region. It patches up the flint church towers and composes the adjoining Georgian and Regency rectories. Early Tudor brickwork, a sign of a fashion from Essex, adorns churches at Wyddial and Meesden—and the Brick House, near Great Hormead, is the real precursor of the county's splendid brick masterpieces—North Mymms House, Hatfield House, Tyttenhanger, Balls Park, Queen Hoo Hall, Mackerye End, and Little Hadham Hall. And some might argue that this developing habit of building in brick, as it spread in a wide band across the south, gave Hertfordshire, despite its reliance on agriculture, the familiar look of one of the Home Counties.

Her stay at Howards End changed Mrs Munt's views a little. No true impression of a county can ever be got from a train window, or from reading about it, or hearing prejudiced accounts. Hertfordshire's man-made landscape ('homely and humpy' is Charles Lamb's description) to some may seen uneventful—many of its churches (St Albans cathedral and Hemel Hempstead being obvious exceptions) pedestrian, apart from the furnishings and often magnificent monuments—its towns and villages places to live rather than places to visit. For the sceptical tourist and the jaded Hertfordshire resident this guide is specifically designed. May he or she discover, as the present writer has done, not only some of the most *varied* countryside contained within the boundaries of any English county, but also Royston's unique cave, the 'world's craziest pub' (at Hunsdon), Tewin's grave-eating tree, Wren's Temple Bar, and other astounding curiosities.

Ovaltine buildings at
Abbots Langley

Gazetteer

The number in brackets following the place name refers to the appropriate square on the map at the back of the book.

Abbots Langley [8] A large suburban colony sloping down to the River Gade from the old 'village' on the edge of the countryside. North of here the thatched and half-timbered model *dairy* (1931) of the Ovaltine Egg Farm looks like a Disneyland set. Way below is the Gadeside factory turning out the bedtime drink. At *Bedmond* in the late 11th century was born Nicholas Breakspear, the one and only English pope (Adrian IV). Two hospitals and an aerodrome divide Langley's suburbia from that of Watford. *St Lawrence's church* looks an orthodox Decorated and Perpendicular building from the outside with chequerwork and tracery (especially spiky sort in the chancel). The surprises are inside: a most Cotmanesque Norman arcading of zigzags and billets as at Hemel Hempstead, but with later foliation on the south arcade capitals. Look diagonally across at them from the corner of the south chapel, which is Perpendicular, open to the chancel, and has a crude contemporary wall painting. Disturbing monument here to Dame Ann Raymond (d. 1714) shows her sitting in a cavernous niche. Beneath are three cots symbolizing the babies that died 'within few weeks after theyr Births'. In the nave there is a life-size, life-like marble Robert Raymond (d. 1732) signed by Cheere. Georgian vicarage. South-east of the church a suburban village shopping street develops a distinct country-village character, if only for a hundred yards.

Albury [6] Spread-out parish with three population centres in typical East Hertfordshire country. The old centre is on high ground half a mile west of some newer development at Clapgate. *St Mary's church* has a miniature grandeur. The 13th-century chancel contains some very ordinary Victorian woodwork, a medieval screen of most tendril-like tracery, and some unusual Art Nouveauish brass plaques among the ancient ones. A whitewashed and clear-glazed 14th-century nave retains some original window tracery. The stone effigy of Sir Walter de la Lee's wife shows her unnaturally slim. A venerable iron-bound chest is of timber with the quality of fossilized sponge. Extensive views from an open churchyard of a landscape punctuated by pylons. In the graveyard is an exotic flowering of Art Nouveau around the *Shoobridge tomb*: wrought-iron rows of stiff lilies pointing heavenwards under a forest of scrolls, pinnacles and intricate grillework; speckled verdigris against the deeper green of the lime-tree avenue behind. A house called Labour in Vain was once an inn. The village pond is said to be as deep as the church tower is high. At *Patmore Heath* (1 m. NE) is a nature reserve with some cottages dotted around its fringe, and Patmore Hall, half-hidden near the site of a deserted medieval village. On a misty morning the woodland of lanky hornbeams takes on the look of a Rowland Hilder water-colour.

Aldbury [4] Film-set village. Under the green whale-back of Ashridge a triangle of cottages surrounds a large pond and stocks. A cheerful old inn, a bakehouse with a striking chimney, thatched and timber-framed cottages along the *Stocks* road make for a harmony of brick and whitewash and gleaming paintwork. The *church* (St John the Baptist), ordinary Early English and Decorated, houses a splendid Perpendicular stone screen. This guards the Pendley chapel and its monument of two effigies to Robert Whittingham (d. 1452) and wife. His feet rest on a wild man clutching a staff and hers are on a hart. There are medieval encaustic tiles in the floor and a few attractive brasses. Stocks, on the Buckinghamshire border, was the home of the now unread novelist Mrs Humphry Ward (1851–1920), granddaughter of Rugby's Dr Arnold and mother-in-law of historian G. M. Trevelyan, who often stayed there. George Bernard Shaw was an occasional guest at Stocks cottage, beneath the hanging woods. Aldbury is plainly the Clinton Magna of Mrs Ward's *Bessie Costrell* (1895). The mid-Georgian mansion, remodelled by the novelist is handsomely screened by trees. It was once owned by the chief executive of *Playboy*. In the farmyard opposite is a chequered brick dovecot with its date of 1753 picked out in blue headers. Tudor Cottages and its long barn of gridiron timbers make a picturesque group. The Duke of Bridgewater's *monument* is an austere Doric column topped by an urn, and stands in a woodland clearing of the Ashridge estate. Erected by Wyatville (*see* Little Gaddesden) in 1832 to commemorate the Duke's pioneer canal promotion, it has 172 steps to a viewing platform and is open to the public. The road to Tring is haunted by the ghost of Simon Harcourt and his phantom coach—no sights, only the rumble of wheels and reins jingling. Hard by the new Tring station the *Royal*

Aldbury

Hotel of 1838, once a busy 'posting house' (see sign), now rather shabby-genteel, personifies the early railway age so graphically described by Dickens in *Dombey and Son*. Outside is a cobbled courtyard, having a pump with bucket, and the accommodation facing the mews. The 2-mile stretch of railway cutting here on this pioneer London to Birmingham line was often discussed and marvelled over in the popular railway literature of the time.

Aldenham [8] Less than two miles from North Watford are red tarmac lanes of cow-parsley and shapely horse-chestnuts, shaded hamlets of Tudor farmhouses (some playful Gothick), and wide views over woodland and river towards the motorway. *Church* (St John the

Baptist), former vicarage and farm, both Georgian, lie on a loop of lane which was once the main road. A village giant of a church with a lanky tower, having stair-turret and spike heads, a long nave, chancel and chapels. Early English work in the tower and chancel; the rest late Decorated and early Perpendicular. Look at the stately aisle arcading's peculiarly grotesque masks and angel corbels above. A murky nave has stained glass in all its windows but two, and the walls are littered with barely seen tablets. Medieval stairs lead to a Victorian rood loft. One *major monument*: to Crowmer ladies, *c*. 1400. Two stone effigies on carved tomb-chests and under canopies are knit together by an embattled cornice featuring turrets like miniature church towers. Green Men in canopy

spandrels. Each effigy is spotlit from the back by a lancet. Cade memorial (kneeling female in niche) is late (1650) for its type. In the north chapel corner is a life-like marble *tableau* of *c*. 1714 to John Coghill and wife who appear to be debating a point of domestic etiquette. Opposite the church is a long drive through semi-parkland and past pleasant modern buildings and conversions of the present college of education, to *Wall Hall*, now the staff centre. It is castellated Gothick of 1802 and *c*. 1830 à la Knebworth with romantic grounds. *Aldenham School*, near Letchmore Heath, has some castellated bits from *c*. 1825. *Chapel* across the road boasts two paintings by Stanley Spencer, of 1958. *Letchmore Heath* is a cheery red-brick and half-timber hamlet luxuriating

40

Aldenham

in horse-chestnut trees. The mansion was taken over by 'The Society for Krishna Consciousness'. More Gothickism in Wyatville's *Hilfield Castle* of *c.* 1805, with its gatehouse and portcullis. Shades of Walter Scott!

Amwell, Great [6] Here, below the church, is a shrine to the principle of *ut pictura poesis*; a vignette illustration by Westall or Uwins, brought to life by Robert Mylne in 1800 as a tribute to the achievement of Sir Hugh Myddleton, the engineer whose New River of 1609–13 brought fresh water from King's Meads (near Hertford) and Amwell, to Islington, for the citizens of London. In the river the willows and a cypress on two islets shade an urn memorial to Myddleton and a whitened stone bearing

lines by John Scott (*see* Ware) celebrating the nearness of spring water. A brilliant neo-classical tableau. *Church* (St John the Baptist) of flint, a perfect foil to Mylne's artifice, is one of only three in Hertfordshire with a Norman apse. Gloomy and dull interior. The sloping graveyard is a romantic eyeful of *monuments* bristling among yews and cypresses. Mylne's own mausoleum is blockish and white bricked, topped by a pedestal and urn, and plastered with tasteful stone tablets. There is an obelisk and sarcophagus near by. In the village, *Amwell Grove* was Mylne's own house. On back lane to Ware, $\frac{3}{4}$ m NW of church, is a lamppost museum owned and run by a manufacturer of concrete examples. Curious lampposts of all ages and types form an avenue.

Amwell, Little [6] Dour hillside outcrop of stock and raw red brick overlooking built-up Lea Valley. An unmemorable red church of 1863, a school of similar date in a lane of villas ending in woodland, and a tiny green with an old inn. Paths through holly groves to *Haileybury College* (1806–9), by Wilkins, the architect of Downing College, Cambridge, and the National Gallery. Built as training centre for the East India Company, and a school since 1862, it has a long, low stone-faced façade, the colour of rainwashed chalk, with three porticoes inserted. In another side the old chapel, now a library, adjoins a pretty little house (the Master's?) set back behind a cedar. New *chapel* is crowned with a green dome and looks like the pompous bit on a Victorian pumping station.

41

◁ **Aldenham**, the Crowmer Ladies   **Aldenham** church △

Haileybury College, **Great Amwell**

Around the huge green quad is homely yellow-brick accommodation. In the grounds are perversely red-brick ancillary buildings, and there are interminable playing fields. In the grounds of Georgian *Gamels* ($\frac{2}{3}$ m. S. of village) by a dark pond at a lane's end, is a converted stable-block home of Alan Davie —artist, glider and jazz enthusiast.

Anstey [3] Village straggling up and down lanes in barley and turnip country. The general look of this landscape, with its breath-catching prairie views, wind-whipped hill crests, sudden roadside ponds and mysterious moats, is an acquired taste. There are farmsteads and cottages of predominantly white weather-boarding and thatch which are little changed since the 17th century. Near Cheapside is a cottage terrace bearing the monogram 'D' for Dimsdale—a family that still owns most of the land around here. By the stuccoed Hall and farm barns rises *St George's church*, a rewarding, visually stimulating building in which most architectural periods are represented. It is of basic Norman cruciform plan,

but very late—witness the shaft rings on crossing tower piers. The contemporary font, with a frieze of four mermen clutching their tails, has only one rival in England, that of St Peter's church, Cambridge. There is Perpendicular tracery in the chancel, and transepts that were rebuilt *c*. 1300. Tomb canopy is also of this date, as is the arcading of the enlarged nave. The arches have an odd, almost triangular, severity—proof, perhaps, of the builder's inability to cope with the fashionable Decorated style. Clerestories, aisle windows, porch and striking lych-gate are all 15th century. The last seems to be an orthodox timber-framed *building*. Its right-hand bay was walled up in 1831 to form a village 'cage' for drunkards, etc. Chancel misericords may be early, possibly 14th century. Famous medieval graffiti scratched into the crossing pier depict shields, crests, tiny scallop shell, and a Hockneyish horse's head. 'Our ladi holp' is an invocation to the Virgin Mary. Other imagery suggests a Crusade connection, and thus strengthens the theory that stones from destroyed Anstey Castle were used to rebuild the church. The Butterfield animal

tiles are from the restoration of 1869–71. Behind the church is an overgrown mound and partially water-filled moat of a Norman castle. In the last war a fully loaded bomber from Nuthampstead crashed into the mound, killing the crew. Miraculously, no bombs exploded and the church escaped being turned into builders' rubble. Aircraft fragments still turn up where once Roman pottery was discovered. Two other romantic moated sites lie together near the old rectory towards Meesden— black water gleams. A tunnel is supposed to connect *Anstey Castle* with a blocked up 'cave' entrance at Cave Gate (*see* Wyddial), redis-covered in 1904. Legend tells of a blind fiddler who entered with his dog at one end, never to be seen again. The emerging dog smelt strongly of sulphur! The poet Thomas Campion (1567–1619) was born in Anstey.

Ardeley [6] When the elms went, a distinctly ordinary small village remained, which is best approached through woods and parkland by lane from Cromer or by footpath across fields and the grounds of *Ardeley Bury* from

Anstey church and font ▷

Ardeley, The Green

Walkern church. Donkeys graze in the shadow of tree-shrouded Bury, once wholly Tudor and home of Chauncy (Hertfordshire's first historian), now a Regency Gothick castle; extravagantly fanciful. On a smaller scale the broken semi-circle of thatched cottages (of 1917), around a 'green' with well, ideally sited near *church* and pond, is also a striking architectural exercise — this time blending arty-craftiness with pseudo-Romanticism (a tribute to Nash's Blaize Castle?). The architect was F. C. Eden, who also designed the church's fussy rood canopy. St Lawrence's has stayed coolly engulfed in trees. A well-worn path leads to a Jacobean,

sash-windowed vicarage still inhabited by a vicar. The Tudor porch has an interior of strong contrasts: generously proportioned, typically well-lit Perpendicular nave of poppy-heads, roof-bosses and musical angels; and a cramped and dingy chancel stifled with lancets of shrieking glass, of fiddly carving on stalls. Light-oak rood-loft with canopy (of 1928) is an interjection of almost brand-newness in the gloom, and a rare sight. Prevailing 'High' flavour is confirmed by the presence of Renaissance reproduction paintings in aisle side chapels. Monuments include a moving marble tablet to Mary Markham (d. 1673,

aged 24) whose baby, shown in swaddling clothes, soon followed her. There are memorable Tudor brasses and a Chauncy cartouche. At *Wood End* is a hamlet around a rough Green and along a track. It has a plain pub, cottages and farmhouses. Showpiece is the late 15th-century *Chapel Farm* with its fine studding, overhang, and bressummer carved with vine leaves. Disused Victorian chapel was built right on to the farm wall, on the only available plot of land.

Arkley [8] Absorbed into Greater London in 1965.

Ashwell [2] Large village looking like the small market town it once was. Ashwell is popular, expensive, rather chic, and utterly unlike any other place in Hertfordshire. Southern intimacy has gone. There are long, green views over a Cambridgeshire/Bedfordshire plain sewn with woodland and glistening spires. Purposefully pushing southwards, ancient lanes, mud-thick from farmland, tangle and knot with those descending northwards over a thorny chalk ridge, past Iron Age Arbury, around the pivotal bulk of the *church*, whose vast, desolate tower of clunch looms above the roofs like an early skyscraper in old Brooklyn. With the departure of the market and old industries, which included brewing (the Mill Street maltings are converted), and with the lemonade depot and council houses pushed out on to the periphery, Ashwell can continue to mimic the sort of semi-idealized little town created to illustrate a novel by Jane Austen or Mrs Gaskell by someone like H. M. Brock. One almost expects to meet bonneted women and children with hoops around each corner. And yet the beauty is robust. This is no Lavenham or Lacock. There is white South Cambridgeshire brick to offset medieval and later timber framing and plaster in the High Street and its continuation westwards. The *Guildhouse*, *Forresters Cottages*, *Bear House* (featuring

Georgian **Ashwell**

wooden tracery in its plaster) and the *Chantry House* (particularly memorable) all survived the 18th-century fire. Back Lane, running parallel to the south, is a further foil to prettiness—a street of mainly short (and early) Victorian terraces. There is Georgian urbanity only in the townish Jessamine House, the genteel, sugar-white *rectory* and in some altered windows, notably those of the otherwise medieval Ducklake *farmhouse* (clunch work and Elizabethan fresco inside). Ashwell's visual uniqueness has less to do with the buildings themselves, none of which is architecturally special, but more with their variety and uniform quality, and in the way they, with the other components of a landscape, group themselves, either by subtle design or divine accident, into a model townscape.

Vistas suddenly delight, ravish: the most urban *High Street* which dribbles into a country lane with a farm and grazing field; the way *Mill Street* discovers pure countryside for a hundred yards before it loops back into the High Street by the shaded source of the Rhee, the icy spring waters of which were said in 1802 to gripe thirsty horses; the sight of the church clunch and flint glowing against the billowing

Ashwell

Through the lych gate, **Ashwell**

greenness of the meadow trees. There are curiosities, too: a tiled and barge-boarded butcher's shop straight out of Edwardian London; a square lock-up of clunch in Hodwell, itself an odd thoroughfare; a water-wheel perpetually churning the air of Mill Street in a brilliant modern conversion; a thatched cob wall, now a honeycombed home for bees, in *Gardiner's Lane*. St Mary's *church*, otherwise disappointing inside, contains the strangest legacies of all—medieval graffiti mainly of the 14th century, and in Latin. On the nave piers are complaints from an embittered architect and a lover. Under the

tower is a unique and heavily incised representation of old St Paul's with its spire (then England's tallest) looking curiously unconvincing. Round about are inscriptions dated 1350 and 1361, the first bewailing the effects of the Black Death, which started *c.* 1349, and the second reporting a great 'tempest'. On the opposite wall are nailed 18th-century memorial plaques of lead which were once attached to the spire. All around, in the tower, piers and tracery we recognize the gracious simplicity of early Perpendicular. The chalky north and south porches, screen, bench-end carving of griffin and

fierce dolphin, and extremely rare double lych-gate are 15th-century additions. Far less welcome are the water-colours depicting prancing hermaphrodite angels, and the tapestries by a former student of the 'William Morris School'. Thankfully the blue nave window curtains have been removed. Ashwell has a small *museum* (open Sundays only) in the timbered *Town House*, and a craft shop. *Ashwell Bury* is a mansion remodelled unmemorably by Lutyens. Best viewed from road to *Ashwell End*, where local historian Hine and John Beresford, editor of Parson Woodforde's diary, have lived.

Old St Paul's under the tower, **Ashwell** ▷

Ashwell church

Aspenden [3] As at Great Hormead a dried-up stream bed follows the village street and gets deeper as it heads westwards. Streamside properties, many in large grounds, are reached by brick foot-bridges. Old Rectory bridge is decidedly grand. But, unlike Hormead, Aspenden is a backwater, and its main street is a dead end. Leafy setting. There is pargeting and thatch, some dowdy council houses, and some bungaloid growth. *St Mary's church*, well sited on a hillock alone, has a pleasingly

brick-patched and cemented exterior. Chancel lancets show a 13th-century origin, and there are later additions, including an imposing 1525 porch and south chapel of 1622. In the latter a splendid early Tudor *monument* to Robert Clifford and family has a frieze with finials. Another canopied recess of the same period features crockets. Effigies to Ralph and William Freman, two Jacobean gentlemen in ruffs, show them coyly holding hands. In rolling fields one mile south-west a tree-shrouded pond

marks the site of Berkesden Green, part of a deserted medieval village.

Aston [5] A brook divides it from Stevenage New Town—but it is unlikely to follow neighbouring Shephall into the giant's maw. Its commuter residents will not let it. An essentially small village now top-heavy with new housing, both good and mediocre. Facing the *church*, in the grounds of *Aston House*, a close of exclusive, architect-designed homes has the converted William and Mary stables as a

52

centrepiece. It is very chic, very *Homes and Gardens*. The big Perpendicular St Mary's church is also 'tasteful', but ultimately vapid. Craftsmanship is all: moulded roof-beams; cloyingly ornate sanctuary; florid choir stalls imported from St Mary's, Lambeth, to match the ordinary Perpendicular screen. *Aston Bury*, almost hidden down a lane, is a mainly Jacobean house with mid-Tudor bits. Twisting chimneys and ogee gables.

Ayot St Lawrence [5] George

Bernard Shaw's village lies in narrow high-hedged lanes on the edge of parkland. Group of Brocket Arms, diamond-paned Post Office (the setting of Shaw's *Village Wooing*) and cottages, all timbered and Tudor, is idyllic. Old St Lawrence's *church* was only partially demolished by Lord of the Manor Sir Lionel Lyde in 1770s because the Bishop of Lincoln intervened. Nevertheless the roof had gone, and since then two centuries of English weather and ivy have performed wonders. A Perpendicular north tower shoots up white behind the greenery on the earlier main fabric (some Decorated tracery). The north chapel's lavish arch of mouldings and stiff-leaved capitals (damaged) was removed here from the original Early English arcade. Horrible brick buttresses have been added in places; windows bricked up; and stonework defaced or frost-cracked. Leprous Perpendicular effigies of knight and lady, and a murky graveyard. Lyde's new *church* of 1778–9, built to catch the eye from Queen Anne Ayot House across the fields and behind trees, is the best-known building by Nicholas Revett, and most avant-garde for its time. Brick (which is exposed at the back) faced with cement; a portico copied from a Greek temple and reproduced at Trafalgar House, near Downton, Wiltshire; unGreek colonnades flanking; and a cool chapel-like interior of coffering and sunbursts and mini tunnel-like transepts.

More Palladian than Greek Revival. GBS lived at the purple brick, late Victorian '*Shaw Corner*' (formerly the New Rectory) from 1906 until his death in 1950. Ground-floor rooms are furnished exactly as the writer left them—monuments to his baffling idiosyncrasies. At the bottom of the garden is his writing hut complete with telephone, electric fire and bed. *National Trust.*

Ayot St Peter [5] A sylvan hilltop

setting above suburban Welwyn for an Arts and Crafts *church*, Gothic rectory and ex-school. In a damp churchyard of mossy walls, silver birches, cherry laurel, decaying fungi, a cedar and a monkey-puzzle tree, the brick St Peter's of 1874–5 is a-dazzle with red, white and blue decoration. Such fancy work gravitates towards the tower which has a mosaic clock. Period-piece interior features a chancel arch by the famous Martin Brothers, of Southall, designers of grotesque pottery birds and deliberately distorted thrown vases. Architect Seddon also built Chelsea's Rossetti Fountain and the ponderous University College at Aberystwyth, in comparison with which St Peter's is a diversion, a toy. Mineral railway meanders through woodland to giant Wheathampstead quarry.

Baldock [2] A small town with a

big romantic past. When neighbouring Letchworth was common land and cottages Baldock was one of Hertfordshire's premier coaching centres. It was on the Great North Road and also linked in with an important route from Luton to Royston. If big, square archways into courtyards indicate inns, Baldock's popularity, even from Tudor times, can be imagined: half-a-dozen examples in Hitchin Street, as many in the High Street, a grand one by the churchyard in Church Street, a handful in Whitehorse (named after the inn) Street. Some retain their huge heavy oak doors; most are timbered inside; and a few are gentrified to suit the age. But

Baldock's great days are over. The biggest Georgian inn is now a steak restaurant with plastic signs, the High Street's pre-motorway-age snack bar (round tables screwed to the floor) is a period piece, the giant Astoria cinema—a classic 'thirties monument—is now a bingo hall. Letchworth, Hitchin and Stevenage have the big shops, the cinemas, concert halls, theatres, museums, while Baldock sleeps—a rather expensive dormitory. Gone now is the Great North Road, the town's main artery—cause of its success and prosperity —now reclassified and renumbered, its through traffic channelled off into the A1 motorway. And yet lorries and motor coaches stop for the café, motorists for the chic antique shops and a steak. There are stalls on market day, and much amiable bustle. The town plan is a crucifix created by the four streets mentioned earlier, with a church at the intersection. All visitors should enter (or leave) along the romantic old route from London—a wide stretch of gently descending tarmac, a line of Tudoresque villas fronting a Paul Nash screen of trees on a rampart of the Weston Hills. A sharp bend and then the palatial Kayser Bondor stocking factory, hugely grey behind lawns, faces the redundant cinema. But then High Street suddenly opens out with at first 18th- and 19th-century cottage groups and timbered buildings, then with superior country-town Georgian and Queen Anne brick towards the crossroads. A harmony of rhythmic rooflines and inoffensive shop-fronts with the occasional well-placed tree. Among all this the corner *Town Hall* cum fire station (1897), of Arts and Crafts brick and roughcasting, appears totally alien. Straight ahead Church Street, seen from the *church* and, forgetting the railway embankment, is any village street in southern England. No through traffic, plain cottages, some timber framing, hints of colour-wash, a sweet shop, boot

repairer's, old timbered Bull inn. Two-thirds of St Mary's church tower is still smothered in 'Roman cement' and the effect, despite the deeply set Decorated windows, is markedly more Gothick than Gothic (compare Bishop's Stortford). A slim spike on an octagonal grey box pokes skywards. There is a tall porch, and a swathe of stone and flint chequerwork on the chancel east wall. In an almost unspoilt, wide and light, 14th- and 15th-century interior, white arcading shoots up from a forest of plain oak pews. Good late medieval corbels support clerestory roofs. The molasses-coloured screens (including rood) reach across the whole width of the building—a splendid symphony of Perpendicular ornamentation, but relatively chaste. South chapel's miniature vaulting develops into a bulging pediment of vine leaves. Sober

Ayot St Lawrence

◁ Old church (*above*) and 'new' church (*below*)

Bernard Shaw's house... ▷

...and his view ▽

chancel contains a wall tablet to Georgiana Caldecott (d. 1846, aged 21), who is depicted at the centre of a tearful Little Nell deathbed scene. In the north chapel is a rare brass of a shrouded couple, c. 1480, and there are slabs to wealthy malt-sters, erected when malting was Baldock's chief industry. Simp-son's late Georgian brewery was demolished in 1967. By the church Butterfield's rectory of 1870–3 con-tributes idiosyncrasy. Hitchin Street continues along the line of the Icknield Way with endearing 17th-century cottages of timber and colour-washed plaster, then more staid mid-Georgian town houses—an eminently photogenic street. Going east Whitehorse Street is airy, less urban and less architecturally distinguished. Brick mid-Victorian Methodist chapel seems Georgian in spirit, despite its funny turret-like but-tresses. Almost opposite, through a carriage arch gentrified in coaching days, is a brick Elizabethan build-ing (with mullioned window) fronted by four white wooden pillars supporting an overhang, presumably also from the coaching age. At the corner of Station Road is a long L-shaped 17th-century affair with courtyard and porch and looking shabby. Incidentally the name Baldock derives from the word for Baghdad given to it by Knights Templar in the 12th cen-tury.

Barkway [3] Large former coach-ing village in good barley country south of Royston. In 1801, at the height of the coaching era, Bark-way was accounted a town along with Hertford and St Albans and had more people (699), more inns (6), and more shops that it has now. Its magnificent main street—two-thirds of a mile long—has a pub and two garages at either end, and lanes and footpaths leading off. It is decidedly townish, and more East Anglian in character than its near-est rival at Much Hadham, with brick and flint, plaster and thatch,

half-timber and Georgian red brick. Of special note, starting from the north, are: late 14th-century hall house featuring a smoke hood inside (opposite inn); early Geor-gian *Red House* with a fine doorcase in an urbane brick front facing the street and a plain country Georgian rear facing the fields; a pair of three-storey ex-coaching inns with carriageways and stabling (facing Church Lane); a widening of the High Street to form a market place—cropped lime-trees now, village pond opposite. On the east side are funny little 'slipper baths' of white brick, dated 1867, and then the prettiest stretch of street follows—a curve of cottages on one side, including National Trust *Berg Cottage* and an endearing Wealdean type, visually set off by the banked trees of *Ashgrove* on the other side as the street straightens. Farther south, Gas Lane contains the remains of an early 19th-century retort gasworks (last village gas-lamp removed c. 1940, since when High Street has been without street lighting). Take the footpath north of Ashgrove for an unusual view of *Manor Farm*, church, and vicarage in an intimate group among trees, but dwarfed by the two distant aerial masts looking uncomfortably close. Manor Farm seems all Dutch gables and Arts and Crafts diamond paning, but conceals a medieval structure. There is a moat and an impressive aisled barn. The unwieldy *vicarage* of 1882, built by its vicar, once had vast grounds. The church is disappointing—big and spreading but almost rebuilt by the Victorians. Original Early English chancel lancets, with some Perpendicular tracery and intact 15th-century aisle arcades ani-mated by stops carved with grue-some crawling beasts and angel and ?Green Man corbels. In the south aisle window two lights of mainly late medieval fragments flank the remains of mid 14th-century Tree of Jesse; four loops of exquisitely wreathed yellow, a king in each, against mocha-brown

ground. Orchestral angels are etched between the tracery above. Chancel monuments include four typical Queen Anne affairs—tall, narrow, much sugary alabaster carving, one with barley-twist columns. Another monument is to Thomas Smoult (d. 1707), a former Barkway vicar. Purposely placed under the tower is a bust of Admiral John Jennings (by Rysbrack) amid cannon, flags and putti. There are some minor monuments. *Barkway House* was visited in the 1840s and '50s by *Punch* editor Mark Lemon and cartoonist John Leech, both afficianados of the Hunt. Leech based the Jorrocks character of Surtees' hunting novels on a local coachman sketched in church. A prominent High Street milestone was one of many erected between here and Cambridge by Trinity Hall fellows Mouse and Hare(!) from 1725 to 1727. Each bears the college symbol. *Newsells Park* and *hamlet*, a romantic world of chalky fields, beech dells and half-seen thatch, colour-wash and brick, lie between the Royston and Barley roads. The present mansion, in municipal neo-Georgian style, replaces the Queen Anne home burnt down carelessly in the last war. A William and Mary dower house, grand stables, and toy-like 'rustick' cottage, dated 1804, remain. A hill obelisk of mortar-faced brick bears no inscription. At the hamlet road junction is an unusual Great War memorial made from boulder. *Cokenach*, in contrasting flat parkland, is a mix-ture of real (1716 and 1833) and later Lutyens-style Georgian brick. Fine stables and c. 1850 moat. Lonely brick barn towards Nuthampstead has an 1851 date and Clinton (of Cokenach) mono-gram picked out in ventilation bricks.

Barley [3] This largish (population 564) village in rolling chalk and flint country on the Cambridge-shire border had an astonishing

Baldock

reputation for attracting the intelligentsia. Rectors Warham and Herring became Archbishops of Canterbury; other incumbents have held chairs at Cambridge, only 14 miles away. Mr Thomas Willett was the first mayor of New York. Dr R. Salaman (d. 1955) wrote the definitive work on the potato here. His friend James Parkes, a world authority on Jewish–Christian relationships, lived at the Old Granary and housed his vast library in the wooden hut next door. Barley today looks a rather ordinary farming community surrounded by some of the vastest fields of its namesake in the county-prairie downland—a Sussex or Berkshire without sheep. More earthy and less physically grand than its neighbour Barkway,

with less commuters and more council houses, Barley seems to be looking more towards Royston and Cambridge than London. Nevertheless there are some striking individual buildings such as *Homestalls*, first to greet you from Barkway, which is a Tudor building swamped by additions of 1900 and 1913—the latter by Barry Parker of Letchworth Garden City fame. Immediately recognizable Letchworth-type details include tile-hanging, herring-boning, roughcasting and rain-water pipes decorated with vine leaves. Gardens (unfinished) are also by Parker, but the eccentric water tower/viewing platform was not his idea, but that of the owner, potato expert Salaman. Up Baker's Lane ($\frac{1}{2}$ m. N.) is another Arts and Crafts

house, *Dalny Veed* (1907) by Edgar Wood, which is well concealed from the road. The *Fox and Hounds* inn, with a much remarked-at sign (depicting huntsmen pursuing a fox) stretches across Church End, but is not the original pub of that name. This stood in the High Street and was burnt down, together with its famous sign of lead figures, in 1950. In Church End there are some pretty cottages, the unusual *Town House* of *c.*1526 (much altered) which after having been variously school, almshouses and spinster's home, is now the Village Hall. Opposite is the *church* of St Margaret which was almost entirely rebuilt by Butterfield in an utterly lack-lustre style: compressed currant-cake flint exterior, an awkwardly contrived 'spike'

57

Barkway (*left and above*)

Barley

replacing a handsome Georgian bell-cot, and an interior which preserves a Jacobean pulpit and medieval stained glass. Buckler water-colours show what a delightful little Perpendicular church it once was. Facing the inn sign is the sturdy, timbered 17th-century 'cage' for securing drunkards and others. *Smith End* is a winding hamlet with a striking orange farmhouse. From ancient *Shaftenhoe End* there are sweeping views across an empty plain. The lane to Nuthampstead past Abbotsbury climbs, dips and twists impossibly through semi-parkland that recalls Shropshire or the Cotswolds.

Barnet [8] Absorbed into Greater London in 1965.

Bayford [8] A miracle that this woodland parish, sixteen stops

from Moorgate, escaped the speculative development that afflicted Cuffley down the line. A small and unassuming spot which is quietly commuter-dominated. Sweeping prospects north to Mimram valley and *Bayfordbury*'s landscaped parkland, begun in 1763 but with 19th-century cedars and a *pinetum*. The village's oldest houses are on the road to Epping Green—mid-Georgian *Bayford Grange* and *Bayford House*, the latter having exquisite outbuildings. Woodyer's *church* (St Mary) of 1870–1 is plain and neat in its formally planted graveyard. It replaced a building of 1804 which stood on a medieval site. Earlier features retained include a quality effigy of 1612, a Perpendicular font, and a late Georgian fee board. Two heavy iron radiators are rather later. *Bayfordbury*, overlooking expanding Hertford, appears

archetypal Regency, with its stucco and ironwork, but the original brick mid-Georgian house lies in there somewhere.

Bengeo [6] An Anglo-Saxon name meaning spur or ridge over the River Beane. It is a pleasant hilltop suburb of Hertford with some pretty Regency cottages, a grand Hall, and two churches—one Norman, the other mid Victorian. Stuck on a promontory with a panorama taking in the humps and woods of *Ware Park*, the endless water-meadows, and Hertford's rump, St Leonard's is all that a simple Norman *church* should be. It is simply of flint and rendering and consists of nave, chancel and apse (one of only three in Hertfordshire), with the familiar Victorian bell-cot and a cheery Georgian brick porch. The doorways and apse windows are Norman and

Bengeo (*above and right*)

other windows are late Gothic. A cool barn-like interior is cleared of all visual impedimenta. The chancel arch has a crude, skimped, scroll capital and near by is a 13th-century wall painting of the Deposition. In the chancel is a comely lozenge decoration, bold red against white. Wall tablets are few and small. The whole church is so eloquently Cotmanesque. The pale brick of estate housing down a meadowy lane to romantic woodland makes the plum reds of handsome mid-Georgian *Bengeo Hall*, dovecot and garden wall, appear redder.

Berkhampsted castle

Benington [5] In wooded uplands overlooking the narrow Beane valley are timbered and jettied cottages around a tiny sloping green that looks on to the grounds of Benington *Lordship*, with its tree-screened moat, mound and flint folly. There is some innocuous new development down the hill to the east. Adjoining the parkland, St Peter's *church* has rich 13th-century carving around sedilia; 14th-century chapel windows and arcading that has wimpled women on its labels and (horror of horrors!) Edward II shown pierced by a sword; and a 15th-century tower, oak pews and font. The chancel sports lively Green Man corbels. The chapel *monuments* include a much mutilated mid-14th-century table tomb with effigies, and near by, a couple of contemporaries gaze stonily at panelled ogee work. An angel bears tiny naked torsos in a winding-sheet. There are some wall paintings, while outside, a medieval king and others grimace in the gloom. Beyond the formal lawns and rockeries of the Georgian *Lordship* are ponds of writhing life. Nearer the house is Hertfordshire's battiest folly—a neo-Norman flint fantasy of *c.* 1832. An amateurish effort by a landscape gardener, it uses the flint and mortar remains of the castle destroyed here in 1212, but adds a sham gatehouse with portcullis, fake doorways and a shrine for a Buddha to the lumps of ancient walling left *in situ*, ivy-clad among aconite, bluebells and daffodils, which also carpet the bailey. The 'medieval' decoration is laughably toy-like, but endearing. Red brickwork has been exposed where the 'stone' made of Portland cement has fallen off. *Open at times throughout year.*

Bentley Heath [8] In hushed back lanes by the north gate of *Wrotham Park*. A perky little red church by Teulon, a row of Victorian estate cottages and others huddle around a makeshift green with a horse pond. *Wrotham Park*, an unexceptional Palladian mansion by the Burlington protégé and former chimney-sweep, Isaac Ware, was

Berkhampsted castle

built for Admiral Byng in 1754. Three years later Byng was shot for 'neglect of duty' or, as Voltaire observed, '*pour encourager les autres*'.

Berkhamstead, Little [8] Not charming, but enviably sited in the mildly hilly, well-wooded belt between Hertford and the northern subtopia of Greater London. At times recalls north Worcestershire, A bitty main street is redeemed by a neat row of weather-boarded cottages facing the church. Pretty Georgian vernacular in Berkhamstead Lane and Robin's Nest Hill, where Little Berkhamstead House, the village's best, stands—boxy Georgian, but with good stables. St

Andrews *church* is a Victorian conversion of a building of 1647. A panelled door has survived. In a dull and squat interior oddities include the north transept arcade arches and a strange east window by Rosenkrantz of 1919. This designer was an immigrant nobleman who worked in a most individual style. This example is late. Opposite the Elizabethan *Gage house* is *Stratton's Folly* of 1789. In brick, tall and embattled, it contains a spiral staircase of 150 steps leading to a former library and is similar in structure to the 1756 'monument' at Edgbaston, Birmingham. At *Epping Green's Beehive inn* is a pew of 1647 removed from parish church.

Berkhamsted [7] Remembered for its common, school and castle—not necessarily in that order. Graham Greene attended the school (where his father was headmaster) and took long walks on the thickly wooded common; William Cowper was born in the rectory, now demolished; and Chaucer was clerk of works at the now ruined castle. So much for the worthies. On arrival go immediately to the *castle*. From the Norman mound (steps to the top) the town's unusual shape is brought abruptly and sublimely into focus. To the north, above cliffs of moat, is a horseshoe screen of beeches while to the south, in the centre, the ruins are a broken bracelet of flint and

mortar chunks on a bowling-green. Straight ahead is the thin glint of the railway, raised well above the canal and river, its companions since Abbots Langley. Farther back is the school and the *church* and the mile-long ridge of roof-tops that show the line of Roman Akeman Street. On the horizon is the wooded Chilterns' blue blur. From the castle, so close to the action and yet—with only open country to the north—so aloof from it, make for the High Street via Castle Street or Raven's Lane. In the last are cottages, a humpy canal bridge, and vistas of bright canal-side paraphernalia. In Castle Street comely, mainly early 19th-century terraced houses face, on a slope, the brown, dispiriting bulk (centuries of Latin prep, of reeking ink) of the present public school's Tudor grammar school. In its shadow is the graveyard (with gravestones removed) of St Peter's *church*. This grandiose flint town church, added to and interfered with through five periods, has a massive central crossing tower and dominates the most distinguished section of the High Street. A barn-sized but cosy interior, in which medieval features from lancets to clerestory were happily left alone by Wyattville and then Butterfield, who were presumably content to patch up the fabric and pehaps gild a jaded interior. There is no mention of Butterfield's decoration in Thompson's 1971 monograph, so perhaps it was minimal. The latest restoration has resulted in the placing of the sanctuary under the crossing, thus absurdly dividing nave from chancel. The Victorian stained glass is better than average and the *monuments* include chancel effigies of two Jacobean brothers holding hands and an early 14th-century knight and his lady under swaggering ogees. There is a fair collection of medieval brasses. Opposite the church, where the street narrows slightly, interest focuses on the prissily restored *Dean Incent's House* (all leaded glass and gleaming timbers), then the Swan Hotel, Crown Inn and King's Arms, close neighbours in a quietly clever contrast of plaster and chequered brick. From here the High Street slopes mildly eastwards past a large Georgian Red and White House and early 19th-century villas and terraces to track the river through its narrow valley to Hemel Hempstead. On the steep sides to the south there are shoals of desirable Victorian and Edwardian residences in leafy grounds. Westwards are the usual shop-fronts, the mid-20th-century contributions that have flopped, and almshouses of 1684. After a fish-and-chip shop and a garage comes suburbia and Northchurch.

Bishop's Stortford [6]

An important shopping centre and market town serving the rich farmland areas of North-West Essex and East Hertfordshire. On market days (Thursday and Saturday) the town's narrow streets teem with shoppers, while buses erupt head-scarved housewives up from the country. There are auctions for poultry, cattle and antiques as well as conventional street stalls. Stortford is primarily residential and workers travel to Harlow and farther south, even to London. The population has doubled in twenty years and shows no signs of stopping. If Stansted ($1\frac{1}{2}$ m. E.) is developed as London's third airport a town the size of Cambridge will grow up on prime Essex/Hertfordshire farmland, swallowing Farnham and timeless Manuden with it, and more anonymous new estates, like those edging towards Thorley, will appear. Yet the town centre wears its cares lightly and many shop-fronts in long and narrow South Street seem dated and dowdy in comparison with those of Royston, Ware or Baldock, much smaller towns. Potter Street's huge new shopping precinct is not over-conspicuous from the street and was probably welcomed, unlike others. Opposite here the tiny, sloping *Market Place*, overshadowed by Vulliamy's 1828 wedding-cake neo-Classical *Corn Exchange*, lies at the crossroads, a natural hub. Market stalls spill over into wide and airy North Street with its typically country-town Georgian character—quiet brick and plaster and nothing out of place. Water Lane is really a glorified alley running parallel with the street but containing a few picturesque corners and the auction rooms. While Bridge Street plunges down from the Market Place to the Stort, to the ugly new road scheme, to the *Castle* remains that lie in a river-side pleasure garden, the High Street (surely the country's shortest) climbs steeply to the church of St Michael and the medieval Boar's Head opposite, where it widens into Windhill. The tower of this big Perpendicular town *church* is immediately eye-catching— ordinary flint topped with a plum, brick, upper storey decorated by stiff, pedantic stonework. It is of 1812 but looks twenty years younger with a recently leaded spire. In the spacious, whitewashed interior 15th-century features include: poppy-headed chancel stalls with misericords depicting, among other figures, an owl, a swan and a swordfish; a nave (scrubbed roof timbers) and aisles whose roof-supporting corbels are carved with great verve—a hideous monk with a sheaf of corn, a forester with axe, a cook with ladle, and others more difficult to identify, peer down. The usual angels bearing shields accompany nightmarish biblical/mythological beasts. There is a heavy, dark 'restored' chancel screen. Of the *monuments*, the most touching records the death-toll of Mepesden children c. 1686, of whom eight died before reaching adulthood, and seven within one year. Leave the tomb-filled open churchyard for either Church Street or Windhill and from Church Street gaze east across the valley to where All Saint's *church* (of 1937), *Hockerill*, looks perplexingly French among the red

English roofs. Windhill is short but as wide as a market place with well-grouped Regency and early Victorian homes behind pollarded limes, an odd *chapel*, a malthouse and a granary. The porch of the long, Regency stuccoed British Legion H.Q. is falling apart. Then suddenly, delightfully, the town seems at an end and fields and hills are glimpsed through the gaps between houses on Windhill Road; yet to the north Stortford's late Victorian mansions sleep in their leafy grounds. In South Road (going towards Sawbridgeworth) is the white Regency villa where *Cecil Rhodes* was born in 1853, now a *museum*. Behind here, in Southmill Road, are maltings converted into an arts centre. Other maltings, sad relics of an industry moved farther south, around the station area, where grain stores and flour mills now rule.

Borehamwood [8] For years headquarters of the British film industry (the pioneers having arrived here *c.*1913) when there *was* one. Today the MGM studios are a cold store, the famed Elstree studios, built in the 'thirties and now looking sad and shabby, are partially let out to smaller film companies and showbiz ancillaries, and the 'thirties parades on Shenley Road, the boom town's Sunset Boulevard, are indistinguishable from those of Hendon or Mill Hill. There is a whiff of nostalgia in the names—'Studio Parade' and 'Studio Cafe'. A very early movie-making building still stands by the roadside and is now a cutting room. A suburban villa does duty as a props store. Bits of Edwardian Boreham Wood, a 'modern settlement ... of pleasant houses with gardens', shops in Station Parade, and 'Refreshment Rooms', can be glimpsed towards the railway, which cuts through the remaining trees of ancient 'Baram Wood'. A tide of London council housing moves ever northwards.

Bourne End [7] (near Hemel Hempstead). Off the main road in lush Bulbourne valley are cottages on a farm track running along a Chiltern cleft into Buckinghamshire. Conspicuously positioned roadside *church* by G. G. Scott, its stained glass protected by aluminium-framed plate glass. Waste spaces in back lanes are haunts of deadly nightshade and the striking thorn-apple.

Bovingdon [7] Humble cottages jostle uneasily against crude red brick of the 'thirties and 'fifties, seedy shop-fronts, a fire station and a memorial hall. Unplanned aimlessness. Luckily some pretty cottages remain in lanes north of here. Also in the area a *church* (St Lawrence) is best viewed from the edge of Hertfordshire's second largest churchyard—four acres crossed by a soldierly avenue of clipped yews. A building of 1845 by Talbot Bury, designer of Chipperfield's church, it is severely traditional with a comfortless interior preserving a stone knight effigy. Towards Flaunden there is much ribbon development.

Bramfield [5] Quiet, dull village in good conifer country with a shaded Jacobean former rectory by the tiny green. *Church*, said to be Thomas à Becket's first living, has a toy-like brick and cement tower (with spire shaped like an upturned ice-cream cornet) of 1840, a nave cemented over in the same year, characteristic contemporary mouldings and tracery, and a tellingly contrasted medieval flint chancel. It remains deeply and inexplicably melancholy.

Braughing [6] (pronounced Bruffing) A village in two parts. *Green End* is the main road part—an architectural all-sorts from medieval (Old Gables is striking) to modern villadom. From this 'end' a lane plunges directly down to the River Quin (really a stream) and its ford, while two other lanes skirt the opposite ends of the village, discovering vistas of shaded stream meadows, half concealed farmhouses and roof-tops among trees, before they meet uphill from the Quin at the colour-wash, timber-framing and church part. Cottages huddle around this *church* of St Mary, whose tower and spire are landmarks. The style is dignified village Perpendicular, with an earlier chancel. On the spacious porch are terrifying gargoyles and a reproduction sundial dated 1971. The nave corbels are equally hideous. Flanking the tower doorway are niches containing pretty miniature fan-vaulting. In the nave angels bearing scrolls and shields support the roof. Down below the carved farm animals on the benches look too animated to be Victorian! The chancel, approached beneath a firmament of gold and blue stars, houses: effigies of the Jacobean Brograve brothers, who lie on their sides, one atop the other; a severe Scheemakers medallion profile; and a sarcophagus with putti to Ralph Freman, d. 1772. From the churchyard a path leads eastwards to a tiny, informal square of cottages around a green (Clavering in Essex has something similar). *Upp Hall* ($1\frac{1}{2}$ m. SE) is a staid, much-altered early Jacobean mansion. Its truly enormous brick barn is twice the height of a modern Georgian-style executive home.

Brent Pelham [3] Called Burnt Pelham after a 12th-century fire destroyed the village. The Hall's grand William and Mary front (chimney-stacks betray earlier origin) rules this place. Its level lawns and brick walls face the hilltop church, while cottages and farms litter lanes sloping mildly north, south and west. The 14th-century St Mary's *church*, heavily restored and generally disappointing, contains one exciting treasure. An antiquarian has fleshed out the legend of local dragon slayer Piers Shonks by fixing his name and a date (1086) to a most unusual black

Bovingdon

marble tomb slab of the 13th century. Symbols of the four Evangelists—angel, eagle, lion, and bull—are carved in relief around a *dragon's* mouth, symbol of militant Christianity. Surely a fanciful attribution, and yet a huge skeleton has been recovered from this very tomb! *Shonks Moat* (1 m. E.) is a well-defined ditch, now only partially water-filled, with a medieval fish-pond and traces of an earlier moat near by. Samuel Palmer landscape of ancient woods and tracks through swaying corn north of here.

Bricket Wood [8] Deep, dark woods and common land fringed by housing estates between St Albans and Watford. The home of fungi and rare plants. A sinuous lane tunnels through jungle blackness into heathland of silver birches and bracken, and continues to the M1 and suburban *Garston Park*. Victorian *Great Munden House* stands in parkland overlooking the waterlogged meadows of the Colne. It has an odd little ogeed gatehouse. The *railway station* has murals, painted in 1977, depicting scenes from Bricket Wood's past.

Broadfield [3] Of the grand William and Mary Hall, with its double moat, its 'fair garden' and 'pleasant walk double set on either side with lime trees' (Robert Clutterbuck), only some stables, a clock and a glint of dark water remain. The earth dug for the mansion's 60,000 bricks cost a mere thirty shillings. There was a fine staircase, a splendid main doorway, and swans would cruise up and down the inner moat. The present 1930s hall, ornate brickwork and all, mimics its ancestor effectively. In the bedraggled, wispy-wooded

67

Broxbourne station and river

setting is a deserted village and the remains of a *chapel*.

Brookmans Park [8] Exclusive commuter suburb chipped off Potters Bar and dumped in the grounds of 17th-century *Brookmans*, now vanished. Converted stables are now the clubhouse of a golf-course. BBC wireless masts steal the attention for miles around. Farther south the turreted and castellated *Folly Arch*, possibly by James Gibbs and *c*. 1730, marks the southern entrance of *Gobions*, another demolished mansion, and is a most early piece of sham medievalism. Some details recall those of the slightly earlier 'Castle' by Vanburgh in Greenwich.

Broxbourne [9] Like Hoddesdon, Wormley and Cheshunt, it developed after the 1613 arrival of the New River, expanded still further when the railway came in 1840, and now, with its neighbours, is part of the brickish finger pointing northwards into Hertfordshire from suburban North-East London. It is best approached by car from Lower Nazeing in the east, or by walking from the station, or via the wild and wooded lanes entering from the West. From the A10, going north or south, first impressions are not favourable. In the High Road a 'thirties shopping parade and a 'sixties one with an obligatory tower block (*see* Hoddesdon) face council houses. Then,

huddled together as if for mutual support, grimy, battled-scarred survivors from the old main-road village: an early 19th-century terrace, Georgian *Monson House* (with cartouche and inscription dated 1728), a rambling 17th-century farmhouse, and a long, low, scored and scratched pargeted front, boarded-up and oddly unreal, like a ghostly stage set. Behind, the electric-blue roof of the modern United Reform *church* contrasts cleanly. More red-brick villas until the New River blasts a hole to reveal wider prospects of marshes and the dull green Essex hills. Sequestered *Bridge House* and *Yew Cottage*, both with river gardens, must once have stood in open

Near **Brent Pelham**

country. From here return beside the New River to St Augustine's *church*. Its tall, embattled, stair-turreted west tower, through which one enters, is still Broxbourne's most conspicuous landmark. It rears up behind railway bridge blue-brick, is dimly grey through the lime avenue linking it with the High Road, and springs to attention by the river-side. From all directions it defines the expanded village's old centre. The building is wholly restored Perpendicular with early Tudor additions. These include a rare and exciting stone-faced north chapel whose date of 1522 is part of the incised inscription in a weather-gashed frieze of animal heads and corner pinnacles. Built by 'Syr Wylliam Say Knyct', the south chapel, also stone-faced, is of 1476. The south porch is in

classical vernacular style, most cosy. The open but melancholy *churchyard* of yews and cypresses shows flurries of headstones beneath the spreading branches. An unremarkable interior is dominated by three colours—orange (Victorian woodwork), off-white (stonework and marble-crowded walls) and blue (sanctuary carpet and altar cloth). Two striking *monuments*: an atrociously carved 1609 marble affair to Henry Cock features children, all with abnormal development of the frontal skull; two 15th-century brasses on a tomb-chest have rubbed-in red patches the colour of jeweller's rouge. One of the nave tablets is to John McAdam the road builder. Another depicts horribly real skulls, bones under an angel's wings, and a pick and shovel.

Facing the large green are some stucco and brick early Victorian fugitives from fashionable North London. Around the corner in Churchfields plainer stucco villas of the 1840s (for railway commuters perhaps?) face their much later counterparts across the street. A strong aura of London. Behind Kingfishers pub the recently patched-up kiln and clay-crushing wheels are the only remains of Pulham's tile-making factory.

Buckland [3] Victim of A10 blight and rural depopulation. With pub gone, school ruinous, rectory sold, and church declared redundant, this tiny hilltop community seems to have lost its identity. But there is much of interest: *Buckland House*, chequered-brick Georgian and sporting an exquisite doorcase;

curious moat, decayed *school*, and cottage with a bosky pond—all in a forgotten back lane. The *church* (St Andrew) is a remarkable building, built, apart from 15th-century tower and porch, in 1348, according to some stained glass, now sadly missing. Most window tracery has survived, both Perpendicular and Decorated. The delightful interior has a south aisle only, and pretty arcading. No pews, no clutter. Light filters through plain and 14th-century coloured glass, warming the Georgian and Jacobean marble tablets, making the brasses glow yellow. At *Chipping* (1 m. S.) a fair was held until 1883. *Pope's Hall* has a dovecot and Georgian brick outbuildings.

Buntingford [3] Small, busy, one-street town on the A10. It grew up partly as a result of the desertion by medieval farmers of their barren, wind-blown settlements in the hills around for the more profitable town life. It was on a coaching route (note the number of big carriageway arches), had a railway terminus, and is now a small-scale absorber of London's over-spill—the population has nearly trebled in twenty years. It has needed a bypass for ages, and has now got one—on its western side. Walking the High Street, its width unchanged since the 17th-century, is an ordeal, despite the architectural high quality. Several Tudor and later buildings with overhangs; a handful of urbane Georgian houses, especially Nos. 84–6, 19, 21 and 71; and a complement of modest early 19th-century cottages as well as the startling *White House*—belonging properly in Cheltenham. Unobtrusive shop-fronts, tea-rooms, and antique shops. At the southern end the High Street broadens slightly on one side with houses and an inn set back behind trees, the Seth Ward *almshouses* (1684), a tiny, three-sided masterpiece possibly by Robert Hooke, chemist and friend of Wren, and then the strange St Peter's

Ruined church of St Bartholomew, **Buntingford**

church, looking like a wayside chapel. Brick, tall and compressed, as if concertina'd. The main building was finished in 1626 and the apse added 1899—an error of taste. Facing it across the river, and built in 1915 to deceive travellers into believing it to be the parish *church*, is the Catholic St Richard's. On the hill ($\frac{1}{2}$ m. S.) Sainsbury's have built their charming distribution depot so that it can be admired from as far as Lamb's cottage at *Cherry Green*, or as near as the green lane to *Owles*. The latter is a boxish, embattled Victorian manor lost among trees and with fragments of an ancient moat. Two stone owls stand sentinel on mossy brick piers.

Reached via Church Street, climbing from its shaded river-side cottages, is the ruined *church* of St Bartholomew. Once belonging to the deserted village of Layston, this served Buntingford until St Peter's arrived in the town centre. A 1901 Griggs sketch shows its roof buckling and its south wall cracking. Today the 15th-century nave licked clean of monuments, of identity, is paved and roofless. Winds whip through the staring windows. Everything is stuffed into the still used 13th-century chancel. Leprous Perpendicular stonework in the porch and gaunt tower and waist-high grass in a rambling graveyard. In the new extension is

Seth Ward almshouses, **Buntingford**

the curious grave of Claud Lovat Fraser, miniaturist, book illustrator and Buntingford man, who died young. The elms also have fled.

Burnham Green [5] Supertax Surrey in Hertfordshire. Cut into sandy-soiled woodlands of rhododendrons, silver birches and young oaks are private roads of 'dream homes' in open-plan gardens.

Bushey [8] Watford's posh neighbour. It is a village grown to the size of Hitchin. Along the routes to Elstree and Stanmore are sprinkled

elegant Regency villas, and the odd older cottage or contemporary terrace among the staple diet of flashy Victoriana, Edwardiana and suburban estates. The accent is on trees. Vast schools in big grounds separate it from Watford, and the famous *Bushey Heath*, equal to Hampstead's and the haunt of fungi and rare plants, buffers it from outer London. A visitor of 1806 wrote ecstatically on the prospect from this common: 'On the one hand, is a view of St Alban's, and of all the space between, which appears like a garden; the enclosed corn fields seem like one parterre;

the thick-planted hedges resemble a wilderness; the villages interspersed appear at a distance like a multitude of gentlemen's seats. To the south-east is seen Westminster Abbey; to the south, Hampton Court, on the south-west, Windsor, with the Thames winding through the most beautiful parts of Middlesex and Surrey.' (*The Ambulator*). Thomas Hearne (1744–1817), the topographical draughtsman and water-colourist, whose outlines Turner got 3s. 6d. a night for copying at Dr Munro's, was buried in Bushey. In 1908, with Hubert Herkomer as a leading

72

citizen, it was advertised as 'a favourite residential place for professional and artistic people' (*Where to Live Round London*). In 1873 Herkomer arrived from Bavaria via Southampton Art School and set up home in a roadside semi somewhere near the present Rose Gardens. An informal painting school of mainly local pupils eventually developed into an affair of sixty-two specially designed studios, a gallery and workshop, all designed and built by the painter, his family and enthusiasts in a spirit of Germanic resolution tempered by a communal aesthetic akin to that of the early Arts and Crafts movement. Opposite the remaining studios in Melbourne Road is a barn-like weather-boarded building lit up by a Bavarian woodcarver's frieze dated 1886. Farther down, the British Legion has a unique entrance, the gatehouse, which is all that remains, of Sir Hubert Herkomer's own palace of *Lululaund* (1886–94). H. H. Richardson, American architect of railway stations and court-houses, provided elevation drawings in exchange for his portrait by Herkomer. The resulting schloss was straight out of a Grimm's fairytale—a fantastic alchemy of Romanesque and European High Gothic forms. The interior of mainly woodwork carved by the painter's kinfolk was as heavy and Germanic as the exterior was playful. Large chunks left from the destruction of 1939 lie around the surviving gatehouse-style entrance of Munich tufa and intensely red sandstone slabs. Herkomer died in 1914, having become Academician, Slade Professor, Knight, and having painted Chelsea pensioners, peasants drinking beer, and over 400 boardroom portraits. *Our Village*, probably his best painting, shows the green, church and pond of his Bushey caught in a Vermeer stillness. Little has changed. There are stuccoed, wistaria-clad cottages and others facing the pond. St James's *church*, though dully Vic-

Lululaund, **Bushey**

torianized inside, features an unusual Royal Arms on a beam, a superb canopied pulpit, and two collages of medieval stained glass.

Bygrave [2] Small, dispersed hilltop place of no special character. Population is in the brick villas of isolated *Bygrave Common*. Clear views over three counties. The ditches and banks around *Manor Farm* are odd. Perhaps the work of Ancient Britons, they were waterfilled by the manorial lord in the 15th century. *Church* (St Margaret), approached down a dead-end lined with farm buildings, has a Norman nave with original doorway and a later chancel. The whole is clad in roseate cement (as at Newnham) which glows in the sun. Against the nave wall a delectable stair-turret balances a crude, timber bell-cage. Crumbling clunch tracery. Inside are *Instruments of Passion* on the font and a wooden goose perched on its cover, a rarish wrought-iron hourglass stand fixed to the pulpit, poppy-heads, and poor wall paintings.

Caldecote [2] One of Hertfordshire's smallest parishes—325 acres of bleak upland on the Bedfordshire border. Off a bend in a deserted lane are a big farm, farm cottages, and a derelict *church* dwarfed by gigantic timber-framed barns collapsing into wood pulp, their thatches like sodden, shredded wheat. From the graveyard mess of brambles, tottering headstones, nettles, tree-stumps and fertilizer bags, the church arises emphatically. Of the 14th century, and built with clunch and flint, it is small but delicately proportioned. The roof is propped up internally and the locked porch houses the county's best holy water stoup, a canopied and crocketed affair which is now as green as an alien being. It is liable to dissolve into a heap of beautiful medieval moist chalk. Fifteenth-century features include a font carved with *Instruments of the Passion*, and benches. Excavations near by have uncovered medieval farmstead foundations, and Roman coins have also cropped up.

Caldecote

Chesfield [2] At a muddy lane's end, near the trim 17th-century *Manor House*, stand the ruins of a 14th-century *church* partially demolished by ecclesiastical authority. Jagged flint and clunch walls with window and door shapes pierce green waves of elder-bushes and armies of nettles. Note the Victorian graffiti on the clunch window-sill. Less well known than *Minsden chapel*. The old village has shrunk almost to nothing. E. M. Forster knew the romantic 'Chisfield' Park, its lodge, and the lanes writhing through chalky woodland. It is the landscape of his childhood.

Cheshunt [9] There are two Cheshunts, two worlds. On one side of the A10 a bulging section of the brick-and-mortar curtain linking London to Hertford along the Lea valley—a world of yellow, late Victorian terraces, of seedy corner shops in Station Road, and brash new parades encircling a roundabout featuring a fountain that wished it were in a New Town somewhere. A world of tudor bungalows and newer estates and acres of glasshouses by the railway. The old London road (A1010) was ribbon-developed from the 18th century onwards, and thus must be regarded with an open mind. Going south from the roundabout, a Georgian villa, a Regency Masonic Hall, a few early Victorian villas and a Dutch gable, are shining surprises. Cheshunt's other world, that of the old village gathered around a flint church, lies, half-hidden, to the west of the A10, unbeknown to most speeding motorists. It is best reached via College Road, itself crammed with remnants of old Cheshunt—the cloyingly pretty *Grange* cottages, the near by *Cheshunt cottage*, with barge-boards, hood-mouldings, the neo-Elizabethan treatment of a 17th-century core, and a plain Georgian farmhouse, are striking. Over the A10 and then Myddleton's New River (a vital feature) College Road meets Churchgate. The former *Cheshunt College* is a complex of yellow Victorian 1870s ostentation around a Georgian nucleus. It rather bullies the nearest village rivals of Regency *Church House* and *Green Dragon* inn. Down narrow and twisting Churchfields are pretty village vistas and the gabled and mullioned *Dewhurst school*, dated 1640 and *still* the village school. St Mary's *church* is grand village Perpendicular with late Victorian 'restoration', including some by Bodley. His red and gilt Gothic organ case is sharp against the whitened walls of a most light and airy interior. High wall tablets catch and absorb sunrays filtering through the clerestory. Sober tomb-chests, one with

74

Bygrave

curtains pulled back to reveal the inscription. A gracious church. James Ward, arch Romantic painter of muscle-bound animals, and of the sublime *Gordale Scar*, retired finally to his cottage off Park Lane in *c*. 1841. Both it and its successor are gone, but the near-by thatched and shell-faced lodge (to the demolished Cheshunt Park) survives from the Picturesque Age. North-east of the church is a burgeoning housing development for 6,000 people. It is 'tasteful' and well designed and totally wrong where it is.

Childwick Green [5] Pronounced 'Chillick'. A mid-Victorian 'model village' set in the romantic parkland of *Childwickbury*. No more than half-a-dozen homes around a minute, immaculately kept, white-railed green with a central well. The plain brick *chapel* is by Gilbert Scott, who also refaced the park's mainly 17th- and 18th-century mansion in 1854. The main road *lodge* is a brash display of crimson brick and yellow terracotta dated 1897. On the left going south notice a rare early-19th-century cast-iron milestone.

Chipperfield [7] Dishevelled Chiltern place spoilt by messy twentieth-century development, but redeemed somewhat by a fine wooded *common* and an early-Georgian fronted *manor-house*. At the crossroads, inn, church and brick cottages face on to a small, square green, seemingly cut out of woodland. St Paul's *church*, built 1837, when the village was still a hamlet of King's Langley, is the size and shape of a huge flint barn. Oddly impressive interior, looking later than its date. A powerful organ and equally loud stained glass by Hayward. On the common edge, Apostles' Pond is encircled by lime-trees representing Christ's followers. Footpaths abound.

Chorleywood [7] Metroland epitomized. Chiltern woodland, a large breezy common with a golf-course, a *church* by Street on the old main road, 'many nice middle-class houses' (*Homeland Association Guide*, 1908), including some by Voysey, 'The Orchard' being his own. Explore the Swillet/Shire Lane quarter on the Buckinghamshire border. House prices are astronomical. Ironically, the early socialist Feargus O'Connor established his Co-operative Land Company colony of modest semis at Chorleywood's Heronsgate in 1847. Most have been suburbanized since.

Clothall [2] Big Georgian-fronted farmhouse, perfect Georgian former Rectory, tin village hall and former village school are sprinkled among trees in a steepish lane climbing to Weston. Former village inn, down the lane from the telephone-box, is now also a private house. Parish population has always been tiny, despite length of area covered (from Baldock's suburbs to Walkern). Look at the small number of stalls in the *church*. This is built on a natural grassy mound with prospects over severe contouring of livid greens towards the Ancient British strip-lynchets near Clothall common; a landscape recalling Herefordshire. A no-nonsense but personable 14th-century church of brick-patched flint and rendering. The short tower does duty as a porch. Also 14th century is the south door (preserving ironwork), the south chapel with its window of copybook ogees, and the plain, perhaps crude, roof timbering. The greatest treasure is the glass in the chancel window—rubied canopies and six roundels depicting Christ, the Virgin and Apostles, all set in a field of strutting or flying birds that appear to include a parrot (incredibly), curlews, pigeons and ducks. Luscious 15th-century work, and possibly unique in England. However, similar birds have been seen in a tessellated pavement at Delphi in Greece. There are also a square, worn Norman font and some fragments of brass.

Codicote [5] Unhappy mingling of suburb and village, reflecting enormous growth in recent years, and facing parkland of late Georgian *Codicote Lodge*. Brick cottages and a strikingly overhung George and Dragon inn lead into an oppressively red, urban, High Street. Late Victorian and Edwardian villas; hair salons; car showroom; two grim red chapels. *Church* (St Giles), away from the village, near Bury and new housing, has an Early English arcade, but is otherwise dully restored. The churchyard slopes into a curious hollow. The *Bury* is a 1655 square box with stylish pilastered doorway. Its dignity is killed by a block of flats at the rear.

Collier's End [6] Weatherboarding and timber-framing, a garage and an old-world butcher's shop straddle the obnoxious A10, south of Standon, its civil parish. In the minute brick *church* of 1910 are walls of mouldering biblical prints, a brilliant display of Art Nouveau-ish woodcarving, and a toy-like chancel. Much low-key period charm.

Colney Heath [8] Mild subtopia, luckily in sight of the magnificent *North Mymms park*. Yellow-brick St Mark's *church* (1845 and Transitional Norman in its details) has porch steps leading to the clock tower, and three 1925 windows of radiant Pre-Raphaelitesque glass.

Cottered [3] Astride the busy A507, but because of its plan it remains quiet and unspoilt. In the main street buildings are set well back on both sides behind wide strips of grass (much wider on the north side) with the main road raised slightly above them. Some of the north-side buildings are well below road level and half-hidden among hedges and trees. Throughout the village trees play a vital

ARE NOW CARRYING OUT URGENT
REPAIRS & RENOVATIONS

To Save This Fine
Seventeenth Century
Post Mill
AT A COST OF OVER £7000

Digswell House by S. Wyatt

visual role. Architecture is from terrace cottage to Victorian mansion. Half-way down the south side of the main street the *Lordship*, pink-plastered behind a clipped hedge and short lime avenue, is claimed to be Hertfordshire's oldest inhabited house. *Church* (St John the Baptist) in the angle of the village's Y-shape is externally imposing but internally cold and pompous. Of 14th-century origin, but highly restored, it has a roomy nave with Dulux-white walls, few monuments, and a curious arch into a 'redundant' chancel. After a heavy, oak entrance door the best feature is a large nave wall painting by a village Bruegel of *c.* 1400. Featuring St Christopher it also includes a castle, cottages, manors, a church, and spires—the finest time-capsule. In the grounds of *Garden House*, opposite the church, are 6 acres of *Japanese gardens* created by a wealthy china mer-

chant, Herbert Goode, from 1905 to 1926. Rock-gardens of exotic shrubs, waterfalls, stone lanterns, pine-glades, and a tea-drinking hut—an alien world of symbol and artifice. *Open occasionally to the public*.

Cromer [2] Hamlet of bungalows and cottages on the main road between Cottered and Walkern. There is a square timber-framed *'granary'* by the roadside and on a hill to the east a white weatherboarded 18th-century *post mill*, which has a red-brick round-house, sails and a fantail. Recently restored. *Broom Farm* at *Hare Street* has a shiny William and Mary chequered brick farmhouse and dovecot (with doves).

Cuffley [8] A wooded hillside built up in the 'twenties and 'thirties into a station-centred commuter haven, with half-timbered shopping parades and bungalows. The 'sixties

building jars the period composure. Stockbroker's Tudor lines the route to fungi-haunted *Northaw Great Wood*.

Datchworth [5] A well-heeled parish seemingly composed of many 'greens' littered among a tangle of lanes, but no real village as such. At *Datchworth Green*, the hub, a whipping-post looks awkward in the company of benches, bins, swings, a tennis-court, and an avenue of cherry-trees. All Saints' *church*, though much-loved and cared for, offers little but atmosphere and a few delights: delicate floriated capitals on Purbeck shafts in Decorated north aisle arcade; a brilliant High Perpendicular font that is all panels; and a foliated tomb slab in a recess. White Horse Lane links Woolmer Green with Burnham Green and is said to be haunted by a headless white horse. Pub sign is frightening.

Digswell viaduct

Digswell [5] The breeziest spot in
Welwyn Garden City. Down in the
valley old cottages cower under the
arches of the colossal brick viaduct
built by Lewis Cubitt in 1848–50 to
take the Great Northern Railway
into the King's Cross terminus he
would later design. On the hill,
church and House, matched in
magnolia, lie together looking
south on to communal parkland,
and north on to newish suburban
housing climbing down the valley
sides. *Church* presents a cemented,
rather prettily Gothick north side,
but an early 'sixties addition has
swollen the south side and affected

the interior too. Preserved here are:
some Decorated tracery embedded
in the north wall; mid-Tudor oak
screens; excellent brasses, mainly
15th century, and stained glass by
Eginton. Over-tended churchyard.
Digswell House, now an Arts
Centre, has a huge portico and is
glimpsed to great effect through the
gaps in the houses to the south.
Dick Turpin haunted the ancient
hollow way of Monk's Walk leading to *Sherrard's Wood*.

Eastwick [6] Small collection of
mainly estate cottages in the
meadows of the Stort and facing the

factories of Harlow New Town.
Many of the cottages, the Lion inn,
and a former school are dated.
Most are mid Victorian. *Church* of
St Botolph, extensively restored by
Blomfield in 1872, keeps its
medieval tower with a shingled,
stumpy spire. Inside, ignore
Blomfield and marvel at a 13th-
century chancel arch that has green
Purbeck marble piers. The tower
houses arguably Hertfordshire's
best mid 13th-century effigy—
a crusader in blue-stone with
crisply carved chain-mail around a
leprous face. There are *monuments* to
the Plumers (of Gilston) above.

Handsome Georgian headstones in the churchyard.

Elstree [8] Small hilltop community severed by the boundary with Greater London. On Watling Street the shaded group of weather-boarded cottages, and the brick Hollybush inn facing a Victorian church, is a flash in the windscreen. To the south is the M1 and the Northern Line suburbia of Edgware and Stanmore. To the north and west lie large tree-bounded reservoirs and parkland, enclosing the much remodelled *Haberdashers' Aske's school* (William and Mary and pompous mid-Victorian) and Butterfield's *Home Farm*. Eastwards are the film studios of Borehamwood. Dull St Nicholas' *church* of 1853 replaced a medieval one which had a weather-boarded tower. Preserved are: some piers; a pretty Perpendicular font with its lead piping revealed; and an unusual alabaster tablet of 1603 having an epitaph which babbles about Noah's Ark and doves. There are graveyard epitaphs to the murdered William Weare (*see* Radlett) and Martha Ray, a nobleman's concubine shot by an admirer in 'a fit of frantick jealous love' (Boswell's words) in 1779.

Essendon [8] Seems built in a woodland clearing high above the Lea valley. Apple and cherry blossom in cottage gardens, and climbing plants over brick and plaster. An old inn called The Salisbury Crest faces cottages featuring this heraldry, as does an old rectory. The Salisbury family own near-by *Hatfield House* and park. St Mary's *church* was pompously 'restored' in 1883 and had its east end bombed by a Zeppelin in 1916. An old photograph shows how Georgian box pews, the ceiling, and a panelled chancel arch made way for pattern-book Gothic Revivalism. An exquisite black basalt Wedgwood font on an original neo-classical wooden stand, given in 1778, somehow survived. Near-by brass to William Tooke (d. 1588). Robust 1664 tablet to William Priestley. White-iced *Essendon Place* (now an Electricity Board training centre) is a Regency pile whose terraced grounds of exotic trees and shrubs face those of *Bedwell Park* across the road. *Camfield Place*, where Beatrix Potter used to stay as a child, was later described by her as 'the place I love best in the world'. It is now the home of romantic novelist Barbara Cartland.

Flamstead [5] Urban hilltop village built around an impressive church and now overlooking the loathsome A5 and M1 roads. Much new and old red brick and a dormitory for Luton. St Leonard's *church*, restored in the late 19th century, but retaining features from Norman to Georgian periods, stands in a large, rather towny, churchyard, and has a most visually beguiling interior. Leaves sprout from nave arcade capitals and a large and lavishly carved Perpendicular screen, featuring grimacing jesters among its motifs, almost blocks a view of the chancel. There are wall paintings of varying quality and interest—a skeletal

Flamstead (*left and right*)

Rysbrack busts, **Great Gaddesden**

Death gesturing to three Chaucerian noblemen is memorable; most others are religious. Much graffiti on the nave piers. Stunning marble *monument* of 1690 shows child attendants looking as if modelled in Parian ware.

Flaunden [7] Tiny Chiltern crossroads place. The *old church* is nearer Buckinghamshire's Latimer than Flaunden village. Of medieval 'Greek Cross' plan, now only flint fragments remain in nettles at the spinney edge, 50 feet from the River Chess, the county boundary. No evidence of deserted village site. *New church* of St Mary Magdalene (1838) by 27-year-old Gilbert Scott is the first of 700 or so in his career as hack architect and vandal. Simple Early English nave in flint and brick. Like a Methodist chapel.

Cool interior absorbs colour splashes of John Hayward window, biblical texts and calligraphy. There are elegant pine pews, the *old church*'s font, and also plans, sketches, and historical detail. A third of the parish is woodland.

Frogmore [7] Jaded trunk-road hamlet sandwiched between *Radlett Aerodrome*, river, and railway line to Watford. A little light industry, some plain cottages, whitened, Georgian *Frogmore House*, *almshouses* and Holy Trinity *church* both of 1842. The latter, with its back to the runways, is an early, not unpleasant effort by George Gilbert Scott. Neo-Norman and of flint with scarlet brick, it has a tiny bell-cot and a cool, contrasting interior of blue and white. Around the apse is a Norman-inspired

arcade featuring capitals carved alternatively with masks of woman or bearded man. *Roman villa* site across the river is well hidden among gravel-workings and marshland. *Moor Mill*, to the south, is a picturesque weather-boarded building looking uneasy in its semi-industrial setting.

Furneaux Pelham [3] In two sections: pretty cottages in a hollow with church and inn; then, after a dip down into open ground and a zigzag, tiny *Rayment's brewery*, council houses and cottages at *Barleycroft End*. Wide views south over common and woods. Violet Lane, an ancient and mysterious hollowway, a green tunnel in summer, is a short cut for walkers, but not for cars. Imposing and rather pompous St Mary's *church*, dominating

◁ **Flamstead**: The Saunders almshouses (*above*) and Vine Cottage, (*below*)

◁ Water End, **Great Gaddesden**

Little Gaddesden △

John o'Gaddesden's house, **Little Gaddesden** ▽

Little Gaddesden church: detail of stained glass by Kempe, and Westmacott cameo

Ashridge college and chapel, **Little Gaddesden**

its 'end', has an Early English chancel, Perpendicular nave and tower, the clock inscription reading: 'Time Flies, Mind Your Business'. Embattled south porch has room over. Inside the church the good features are mainly incidental. The chancel has a decorative panel of big-leaved Elizabethan ?daisies, nobleman and dog. A magnificent court-cupboard near by is carved with a satyr and devil. The south aisle table-tomb incorporates an early 15th-century brass of a couple, the man possibly Robert Newport. Another Newport brass boasts an exquisite Perpendicular frieze in the north aisle wall. Roof of wooden angels was recently repainted in canal-barge colours, under some pretext or other. *Furneaux Pelham Hall* is big, though it was much larger, and features Elizabethan stepped gables that peep deliciously over a high, pudding-like yew hedge. There is a garden of peacock lawns, and lakes with ornamental bridges.

Gaddesden, Great [4] Church, farm, school, inn, and cottages huddle under a Chiltern ridge above the water-meadows of the River Gade. Down to Piccotts End this mere sliver noses through cress, is stepped, budded and ballooned into ornamental lakes and lagoons as if part of a landscaped parkland. At *Water End* one long stretch of water is a key picturesque feature in the grounds of Wyatt's severely mid-Georgian *Gaddesden Place* on the hill above. *Church* of St John the Baptist projects an air of importance, even grandeur. Twin gables of the Early English chancel and early Georgian mortuary chapel push arrogantly forward in a bleak churchyard with a stocky rebuilt Perpendicular tower (and stair-turret) following up the rear. Five crumbling altar tombs queue beneath the chancel window. Much stucco, 'Roman' tiles, and bits of old tracery. In the nave most of the vigorous stiff-leaved capitals are restored, and there is an im-

pressively complete, ungilded and unpainted (thank goodness) 15th-century nave roof. A pity about the ten Edwardian children disguised as shield-bearing angels. In the chapel's Halsey 'Hall of Fame' are family monuments of great quality and flair by Rysbrack and Flaxman, among others. Busts, medallions and obelisks are all 18th century. Chancel memorial to John Halsey is probably the ugliest in Hertfordshire, a waste of marble.

Gaddesden, Little [4] Chiltern parish on Bedfordshire and Buckinghamshire border and mostly taken up by the woods and heathland of vast *Ashridge Park*. Straggling street of cottages and bigger houses in grounds faces directly on to beechwoods. Woodland clearings are peppered with rusticated villas and chalet-type bungalows. *John o'Gaddesden's House* is a 15th-century jewel—timber-framed, with an upper storey, and thickly pargeted—in a fragrant old-

Ashridge, the garden, **Little Gaddesden** ▷

Little Hadham, the screen

fashioned garden. *Manor House*, of stone and newish stucco, is dated 1576 and retains original mullioned windows. Georgian *Bridgewater Arms* appears to be a plain farmhouse turned coaching inn. *Church* (St Peter and St Paul), isolated up a lane, is cement-restored and enlarged by James Wyatt and nephew Jeffry, the Ashridge architects. A dingy interior is brightened by exotic floor tiles and a 'High' east end of swinging lanterns, rich altar cloth and stained glass. Many unusually good *monuments* include: 1669 tablet with quirky, scrolly inscription to Lady Brackley; putti and epitaph by the eccentric sculptor John Bushnell (who did the Temple Bar statues) to 14-year-old Henry Stanley (d. 1670); immodest Bridgewater monuments, including a Westmacott cameo of 1823; and two early-18th-century tablets to young

smallpox victims—with poignant tributes. *Ashridge*, now a Management College, is a colossal palace of stone begun by the infamous Wyatt, builder of Fonthill, in 1808 and finished by Wyatville *c*. 1820. Stylistically it falls somewhere between late Gothick and Gothic Revival. If Trollopian bankers and politicians might be found in Pugin's Scarisbrick Hall, which it looks forward to, then Ashridge would produce a Peacockian pseud or a bevy of spectral nuns from a 'Monk' Lewis tale. Look at the Wyatt chapel with its fan-vaulting inside, and its tower with spire. Around the staircase are statues by Westmacott in Perpendicular niches of monks and benefactors of ancient Ashridge, which dates back as a monastery to the late 13th century. Romantic grounds by Capability Brown and Repton and a ruinous Gothic lodge at *Ringshall* by

Wyatville. *Witchcraft Dell*, near Bridgewater Arms was so named after an incident in which a keeper was murdered by a witch. A neighbouring witch called Rosina Massey often rode through the air on a hurdle.

Gilston [6] Scattered village comprising cottages on two sharp bends of the busy A414 above the Stort, and isolated buildings towards the great house and church to the north. St Mary's *church* stands above a lane going nowhere and overlooks rolling parkland. Of flint, brick repaired, and mainly 13th century, it has a tower with a pretty brick Tudor stair-turret. The north nave arcade features bizarre mouldings inside the arches; south arcades are 19th century. Greatest treasure is the wooden 13th-century screen, with its thin piers amusingly topped by vast capitals.

Little Hadham

One marble *monument* to a female Gore includes a breathless, periphrastic inscription; the male Gore remains 'a Prisoner of Hope'. Father and daughter died in 1659. *Gilston Park* (1852), a dour neo-Elizabethan pile, replaces a mansion that Charles Lamb knew and visited. It is now a pharmaceutical research centre.

Goff's Oak [9] Among glasshouses and subtopia is a little yellow *church* of 1860. Down Halstead Hill an early 19th-century land-owner appears to have gone overboard for late Perpendicular cum early Tudor Revivalism—with stunning results. Behind sweeping lawns *Colesgrove Manor* is a big Georgian house lumbered with straight-headed windows that have ogee glazing-bars. The *South Lodge* buildings are extraordinarily toy-like creations of barge-boards and lattice-windows and dormer dovecots, dated 1833. *North Lodge* is similar but soberer. *Halstead Hill House*, a model Regency villa by an overgrown orchard, also has Gothick windows. The overhung corner cottage seems neo-Tudor.

Plainly the influence of such handbooks as Loudon's *Cottage, Farm, and Villa Architecture* was strong.

Graveley [2] Old Great North Road coaching stop with cottages overlooking a tiny, railed-around village pond, a coaching inn, and other Georgian property. In Church Lane a Wealdean farmhouse and barns are grouped with *Graveley Hall* farm of 1719, and flint St Mary's *church*. In the funereal interior of the latter a clock's muffled tick, a musty hassock smell, and glowing early Gothic Revival

glass, lend atmosphere. Ordinary 15th-century screen. Lane continues eastwards, tunnelling through woods to the groves of *Chesfield Park*.

Great Amwell *see* Amwell, Great

Great Gaddesden *see* Gaddesden, Great

Great Hormead *see* Hormead, Great

Great Munden *see* Munden, Great

Great Wymondley *see* Wymondley, Great

Hadham, Little [6] Watering landscape reminiscent of Darenth valley, the thrombotic River Ash tracks *Hadham Ford's* little street for a while, passing a war memorial opposite a high-gabled farmhouse, cottages, chapel and village pump

◁ **Much Hadham** (*left and below, left*)

Green Tye (*right*) ▷
and Bury Green (*below*)
near **Much Hadham**

('Erected by subscription, April 1880'), until the village proper is reached. Crossroads, cottages and an infamous traffic bottle-neck. Honest Hertfordshire vernacular confronts the sham half-timber of brazen Bridge House. Away on the hillside to the east *church* (St Cecilia) stands down a lane, near a farmhouse. It is flint Perpendicular with slim tower, brick Tudor transept-cum-chapel, and one of the most aesthetically satisfying timber porches in the county. So open and airy, so cheerfully rustic. Headstones are framed by ridged and bleached medieval oak. Inside the church, wood is everywhere: oak and pine pews (a few are box pews), carved panelling and floorboards nailed on to the walls of chapel and nave, the canopied pulpit and chancel screen. The latter is as heavy-handed as a lumbering village craftsman could make it.

Ogees sprout stylized plant forms as a twig does cup fungi. The chancel is severely Victorian from floor tiles to roof beams. Encaustic tiles preserved. Across the fields *Hadham Hall*, now a school, is basically a high-quality brick Elizabethan mansion. Its charms have fled.

Hadham, Much [6] Much visited. A grand, rather prosperous-looking village that is strung out for nearly a mile along one of Hertfordshire's quieter main roads. Its attractions are immediately obvious: an appealing mixture of honest vernacular architecture in the leafy main street—with an occasional jewel; a sequestered back lane which follows a stream past yews and wild plum-trees and has a giant beechwood rampart as a backdrop; other lanes which climb through woods of lilac fungi to look down on the half-hidden village. The High

△ Corbels by Henry Moore, tower door, **Much Hadham**

Street runs from the rambling Georgian (1740–5) *Lordship* in the north to the war memorial at the entrance to *Moor Place* in the south. The buildings in between include the Georgian *North Leys*, the early Victorian *manor-house*, then a short phase of 16th- and 17th-century timber-framed and later cottages, many with weather-boarding, before the urbane mid-18th-century *Hall* supervenes and surrounds itself with a brick wall. The White House has Gothick windows, and, on the same side, *Forge Cottage* preserves an original Victorian shop-sign. After a while the close urban pattern breaks down and there are many more semi-suburban detached properties and fewer groups and terraces. Tower Hill has some brick Victorian almshouses and a single engine fire station. At *Hadham Cross* a housing estate is secreted behind a field.

Hadham Mill, further south, is romantically hidden in trees by the River Ash and has mullions peeping from behind its stucco. Near here a woodland track skirts a vast disused quarry, crosses meadows and ends up in the beechwoods behind Much Hadham church. Big St Andrew's *church* is disappointing after the village. Although having a grand Early English plan there is little of interest surviving from this date. The Decorated piers of the north aisle have carved capitals of screwed-up faces. Perpendicular work includes the clerestory, battlements, fine timbered nave roof and supporting corbels of terrifying beasts (and sceptred king), chancel screen, pulpit and font. The porch has a rich roof of mouldings and carved angels. Quirky modern touches include a rock-garden of spring flowers (in nave), a Women's Institute

Harpenden ▽

quilt presented to Queen Mary in 1935, and, outside, two carved faces by Henry Moore on either side of the tower door. The churchyard towards the river is decidedly Pre-Raphaelitesque, with its primroses and ivy-hung walls. On the northern side *The Palace* was, until Georgian times, the country retreat of the Bishop of London. Somewhere amid that late-17th-century brick casing are traces of a Tudor timbered hall. On the southern side the old *Rectory's* yellow plaster, timber-framing and bowered setting are perfection. At *Perry Green* hamlet is a stone chapel of 1855, some handsome converted farmhouses, and *Hoglands*—the home of sculptor Henry Moore. It is curious that both he and the late Graham Sutherland (who lived at Trottiscliffe, Kent) chose the same type of home, similarly sited close to green and inn. In the extensive grounds behind *Hoglands* are Moore's burnished, elemental forms beside hedges and among apple-trees. *Green Tye* has a much larger green around which are arranged weather-boarded farmhouses. Down a lane a barn has snapped in its middle like a doomed tanker and its timbers are cement-filled, country fashion.

Hare Street [2] Spread out along an important B road. *Hare Street House*, of sober Georgian red brick, is the country residence of Catholic Archbishops of Westminster. On the edge of its grounds, near the crossroads, is an enigmatic, very photogenic, little *chapel*. Motto on its lych-gate is apposite in view of the surrounding barbed wire and locked gate, 'And he shall go out no more'. On Braughing road the former Swan Inn is now a 'tea shoppe'. Genuine lavish timbering.

Harpenden [5] With a population of 27,000, only slightly less than that of Hitchin, this is the classic town-sized village. Though always popular with the Victorians, this 'valley of the nightingales' had all the necessary ingredients to ensure a rapid growth of villadom from Edwardian times: open upland country all around and a gorse-blown common pushing up into a broad village street shaded by limes; fishing on the Lea; golf and racing on the common; fast trains to the City. Little has changed. The racing (distinctly *outré*) has gone and a railway has closed, but the strange mixture of brazen vulgarity and traditional good taste persists. Behind hawthorn brush fringing the common, 'retired grocer's Tudor' rubs shoulders with the real thing in the reconstructed *Flowton Priory* from Ipswich and the wistaria-clad *Old House*, formerly the Bull Inn. *Rothamsted's* pompous neo-Georgian main building near by is no surprise. And even in the High Street which follows, with its trees, its greenswards that were formerly rope-walks, and its few timber-framed cottages and inns, the strong sense of being in an expensive dormitory only 25 miles by fast train from London and having golf and good schools, etc., is never lost. Even in 1901 a shopping parade spoilt the view of the common, and today's chic shopfronts might suit Hampstead 'village' better. Symbolically, *Bowers House*, the street's hidden jewel, had a shopping parade built in its front garden in 1936. Its long Queen Anne front is now totally obscured. Slightly earlier and more conventionally attractive, the *Moat House Hotel* has Victorian and modern additions and its name in very large letters, and with the Georgian *Dene* and half-Tudor half-Georgian *Harpenden Hall* makes up a villagey group on the common's south side. *Church* (St Nicholas) is of 1862, but preserves a 15th-century tower and, on the window-ledges inside, some unexciting early Norman decorative fragments rescued from a local garden. There is an Early English font and some brasses. *Rothamsted Manor* has a mid 17th-century front of Dutch gables and a cupola which recalls that of Mackerye End, 2 miles away. Inside are Tudor wall paintings preserved from an earlier structure and vigorously carved fireplaces plundered from Hoddesdon's Rawdon House. John Bennett Lawes, the pioneer of modern high-yield agriculture, helped to found at Rothamsted what was to become the world-renowned Experimental Station. The estate is a rich collecting-ground for edible fungi and some rare species have been reported.

Hatfield [8] Hertfordshire's smallest and dullest New Town has a well-known Polytechnic, a swimming-pool with the 'largest hyperbolic paraboloid roof in Europe' and, in *Hatfield House*, surely the most bravura piece of Jacobean architecture in Britain. *Old Hatfield* is a clutch of red brick and roof-tops gathered beneath the base of a hill and climbing it, via Church Street and Fore Street, towards the church, old Palace and the newer citadel-like home of the Cecils. Down by the station, where incidentally the best views are to be had, disastrous things have happened to the once romantic Great North Road, Hatfield's main street before the New Town arrived. It has been clinically upgraded into a sort of bypass with a subway and waste site clutter, while to the north, just past the only remaining authentic coaching inn, it disappears into a housing estate to emerge as a forgotten lane. Between the main road and the 'picturesque old dwellings' spared by the planners Salisbury Square attempts to echo the elegant elevations of Fore Street with a display of played out neo-Georgianism. Much was lost to this—a piazza with flower-beds, and a 'sixties tub-shaped Roman Catholic *church* with a spike. Church Street's cottages include one (next to No. 20) which has a rockery path lined with crude model buildings raised on stilts. Park Street, cottage-lined, dips to

The first Lord Salisbury monument, **Hatfield**

take the pedestrian viaduct from station to park. The corner *Eight Bells inn* was the probable refuge of Dickens's Bill Sikes, housebreaker and murderer, after his flight from London in *Oliver Twist*. In the heyday of coaching, and before the second Lord Salisbury banished it from his grounds, the Great North Road ran from Bell Bar, past Millward's Park, through Hatfield Park, the Palace yard and gateway, and down Fore Street, where experimental wooden-block paving

was used to ease the ascent. The early Georgian Nos. 2–4 was once the celebrated *Salisbury Arms* coaching inn. Of the great quadrangled *Bishop's Palace*, begun *c*. 1480 as one of England's first brick buildings, only the western *Great hall* survived the demolition necessary to build Hatfield House next door. The present courtyard ranges, including a gatehouse that closes Fore Street like a medieval town 'bar', are Elizabethan and later. A passage of dour Midland Gothic

Revivalism echoes in grimness the depressing dun-coloured mass of the hall. Inside one recalls Ian Nairn's verdict on Eltham Palace and its Great Hall: 'a perfect example of the ornate heartlessness of much mid-fifteenth-century architecture'. Hatfield's hall, an inhuman barn for an inhuman age, reserves a courtly flamboyance for its windows of rich-hued glass and its nest-like roof of oak and chestnut on corbels of carved bishops. *Hatfield House*, built by Robert Cecil

97

Hatfield House, from the south

in 1607–12 from designs by the rather obscure carpenter/architect Robert Lyminge and by ?Inigo Jones, is unquestionably Hertfordshire's greatest mansion, and one of England's show-pieces. It is open to the public. Cecil, forced by his sovereign to take dowdy Hatfield Palace in exchange for his superb Theobalds, settled politician-like to build an architectural compromise—an old-fashioned Elizabethan 'E' with many modern improvements and much bold, lavish decoration. Contrast the north and south fronts: the north, by carpenter Lyminge, a plain and workmanlike cliff of mullion windows and brick; the south, by architect Lyminge on a spree and incorporating a truly stunning central stone *porch* and *cupola* of Renaissance grandeur by ?Inigo Jones, is a joyful celebration of what plain and moulded brick, stone (and money) can do. This prospect of corner-turreted wings balancing the fine stone detailing of the pilastered *loggia* and *porch* was intended for the London courtiers. A broad avenue approach is partly obliterated. Screening the avenue from the house is a most intricate ironwork set in brick with odd brick towers at either end. The avenue continues northwards through the park. A sumptuous interior includes a screen and *grand staircase* (both 1612) by John Bucke. All rather feverish and overwrought, even vulgar, but undisputable craftsmanship. Victorian redecoration, magnificent carved *fireplaces*. House was badly damaged by fire in 1835 when a candle probably overturned. Dickens allows the murderer Sikes a partial redemption by making him a hero at the fire. Hatfield House was one of the first homes to be lit by the Edison/Swan 'electric incandescent light bulbs' patented in 1879. Centrepiece of the formal gardens are green cloisters of trellised lime-trees surrounding beds of old-fashioned English flowers and a fountain. Blinding colour in June and July. A propped-up mulberry; a Spanish chestnut; a backdrop of copper beeches belonging to the deliberately contrasted woodland area of gravelled paths through giant acacias and chestnuts. There

East view towards the maze

Hatfield House: (*left*) Great Hall screen; (*right*) Chapel gallery

is a walled section of formal walks and grassy panels. Immediately east are long vistas of landscaped pasture and tamed woodland. Horribly stunted, hideously deformed oaks, some leaf-crowned, others barely alive, and many hollow, are remarkable. St Ethelreda's *church*, impressively placed on a hill by the Palace gate, promises more than it delivers in the way of architecture. From a murky cathedral-like interior that seems wholly mid Victorian glimpses of original Early English work (chancel) and Perpendicular (south chapel) are revealed. *Salisbury chapel* dates from 1618 and one monument dominates: that to the first Lord Salisbury (d. 1612), i.e., Cecil. On a huge, black marble slab

born aloft by four figures representing the Cardinal Virtues lies the resplendent effigy by Simon Basyll; underneath, a porcelain-white skeleton is a shocking transfiguration. Effigies also of a 13th-century knight and one William Curll by Nicholas Stone, monumental sculptor *par excellence* and later master-mason to Charles I. A selection of above-average late Victorian stained glass, including a Burne-Jones window of 1894 in the south transept. Unexciting Brocket *monuments* of 1598 and 1612; typical Rysbrack busts and cherubs of 1760. Of the celebrated 17th-century 'vineyard' devised by French gardener/engineer de Caus and others little remains of the fountains, yews and fruit-trees, and

nothing of the 30,000 specially imported vines. Partially glimpsed from the trunk road at Mill Green, *Hatfield New Town*, planned without flair after 1948 by Lionel Brett and others, grew around the pre-1914–18-war 'New Town' off St Albans Road and near rock-faced St Luke's *church*. On the 'thirties bypass there are road-houses, shopping parades, villas, and the avant-garde Comet pub of 1933. The *Polytechnic*, very 'fifties, features work by Barbara Hepworth, Reg Butler and Ben Nicholson.

Hemel Hempstead [7, 8] Hertfordshire's third largest town (population 70,000 plus) after Stevenage, which slightly pre-dates it as a New Town. A household

Grand staircase, **Hatfield** House ▷

(pp. 102/103 and above) Great Hall, **Hatfield** House

name as the headquarters of Kodak, Hemel is dramatically sited. The old town grew up by the Norman church and on a ridge, which is the present High Street, well above the meadows of the Gade. Southwards Regency and early Victorian villas sprang up along Marlowes to take in panoramic views of the blue Chilterns. Humbler terraces of this date line Leighton Buzzard Road. Then, farther south, where the Gade and Bulbourne meet at right angles and foster a semi-tropical meadow lushness to set against a paler backdrop of woodland, came the richer Edwardians. Half-timbered gables pepper the hillside by the railway and common at *Two Waters*, and *Boxmoor* boasts an early Norman Shaw *church* by the white and pink horse-chestnut trees. As at Rickmansworth and Hertford the presence of rough country meadow at its busy, traffic-filled core is the making of Hemel Hempstead. Similar oases, consisting of open spaces and woodland left over from vanished estates, separate and add character to the hilly New Town 'neighbourhoods' of *Chaulden End*, *Warner's End*, *Counter's End* and *Gadebridge*, with their 'fifties housing. Canalside cottages in a shaded lane at Boxmoor; others scattered around with the new. On the eastern side *Adeyfield* and *Bennett's End*, also of the 'fifties, are much larger and lack natural landscape advantages. The new housing becomes dullest around *Highfield* and *Cupid Green*. At *Apsley* the waterside paper-mills have the same visual impact as the sheds of British Leyland at Longbridge. They dominate. Back at the big central roundabout there is an air of a south-coast seaside resort (Bournemouth perhaps), in the flaming chestnuts and the wide roads and the shopping centre glittering behind the exotic shrubbery of the Water Gardens. On a hot day an evanescent tang, of trees and flowers, fills the air. Cool walks and alcoves with benches overlooking a

Hatfield House

thoroughly tamed Gade that becomes at last a long pool with fountain and sculpture. The excellent mid 'fifties shopping centre resembles, in its jovial brashness, the rebuilt portions of, say, Croydon or Birmingham, but is strung along the one central thoroughfare of Marlowes. Going northwards we notice how imperceptibly the New Town shades into the old. The office-converted early 19th-century villas dignifying what was once the route to red-brick suburbia now face a complex of early 'sixties civic buildings (Town Hall cum Pavilion, Health Centre, Dacorum College)—all rather friendly. Ahead, the old town proper is fixed by the silver spearhead of the church spire. Starting narrow, the High Street mildly curves and climbs past an ugly *Corn Exchange* of 1857, with a sort of gallery looking on to the churchyard, then broadens with a row of country-town Georgian houses that are now shops (dates 1730 and 1728) until it peters out into a country road. Alleys and lanes slope eastwards off it, and on the church side a row of buildings is sunk below street level and is reached by steps. Most of the old bow-windows are gone. St Mary's *church*, also below road level and ruling acres of municipal parkland, is Hertfordshire's most complete Norman parish church. The central tower has on each side a pair of round-headed windows and blocked Early English ones below, and three ornamental orders of a magnificent west door are a foretaste of a dazzling interior. Arcades of billet and zigzag arches and capitals, both plain and carved with leaves, rise from a sea of

Victorian oak. Rare contemporary clerestory. The chancel is the earliest part and has the luxury of simple rib-vaulting painted in 1888. One chancel arch capital shows a tiny head caught in a swirl of foliage. All the Norman windows are decorated inside with mini shafts, the signature of money spent on quality craftsmanship. Thankfully there are no big monuments to distract the eye, but there is palpably *wrong* Victorian woodwork, however. An Elizabethan stone porch in Gadebridge Park. In a cottage at *Piccotts End* are important medieval wall paintings discovered in 1953— religious scenes and *c*. 1500. *Open to public.*

Hertford [6] With 22,000 people one of Britain's smallest county towns. Here is *County Hall* (incorporating the excellent County Records Office) on a hillside overlooking the town where the old *Shire Hall*, built by Robert Adam's brother, stands in the Market Place. There are two railway stations, East and North, the former a terminus of minor grandeur turned shabby; the County Hospital; a big bus station; and the County Court. All this dignifying a bustling country town of Saxon origins built around the important junction of three rivers—the Beane, Lea and Mimram (with Rib a possible fourth). Hertford is best viewed from the trunk road raised high above meadows of the Lea or from the path running through *Ware Park*. There are gasholders, mills, old maltings, an alien pink church tower, a railway embankment spanning a horizon shining with new estates, intermittent flecks of water and gashes of green reaching up to yellow terraces. Today Hertford is X-shaped, determined by the main roads climbing out, and the rivers. The old centre, however, is squarish, with a medieval street pattern, but

Hemel Hempstead

few surviving medieval buildings, unlike, say, Hitchin. Also unlike Hitchin, but like other small county towns—Carmarthen, Brecon and Trowbridge for instance—the view from the pavement is one of old-fashioned stolidity, dullness even, certainly provinciality. There are few chain stores but many smaller shops in the short, narrow streets surrounding the Market Place and Salisbury Square. From the former, Fore Street, until the relief road's arrival Hertford's busiest (and most congested) thoroughfare, opens out with pleasant Georgian and early 19th-century fronts, including the memorable *Dimsdale Arms* (named after Baron Dimsdale, the 18th-century physician who inoculated Catherine the Great against smallpox) and Barclay's Bank, and the unmemorable Victorian *Corn Exchange*. At the corner, by the new roundabout, lit by a single, giant sodium light, is *Christ's Hospital School for Girls*. Notice the figures in niches and spot the real William and Mary bits among the sea of Edwardian reproduction. Off Salisbury Square, Bull Plain has a tiny one-man museum, a faintly seedy arcade, and leads to a quaint, muddy, river-side quarter of terraced cottages built possibly for malt or mill workers and now targets for modern gentrification. Across the Beane is a lime-tree walk to Bengeo's Norman church. Hertford's only two *churches* of note are both wholly Victorian, mid and late. St Andrews, of currant-cake flint (with stone spire), a cold, painted brick nave and sugary stonework in the chancel lies at the top of St Andrew's Street. Here also are all the best 18th-century houses (Nos. 2–6, 28 and 52 are special) and the antique shops. All Saints, of grimy pink stone, with its thrusting tower looks a bit of Merseyside High Churchiness and dates from 1892–1905. Before the relief road cut a swath through its churchyard, town and church were directly linked via a narrow lane of pretty terraced cottages. Now it's all tiled

subways. Church interior is aglow with fresh, gritty, pink stone, flecked and banded white. There are arcade piers looking like tubes of sherbet fizzers and a soapy marble reredos. Big, mysterious churchyard of handsome Georgian headstones, yews and scented lime-trees. Going farther west, past the brutal roundabout, Castle Street is a short, unremarkable backwater with one striking gabled and pantiled building (No. 23) and an old inn. Of famous *Hertford Castle* little of historical interest remains. Formal lush gardens within the high, creeper-festooned Norman curtain walls; a postern gate; and, lapped by the Lea waters, the original motte. From a distance the gatehouse recalls Hoddesdon's Rye House (q.v.). Of brick, of similar mid 15th-century date, but with extensive Georgian remodelling. Rented by the town council for $12\frac{1}{2}$p a year and open to the public once a month. Reached via another subway, West Street is worth visiting because it's so typically an East Hertfordshire unspoilt town street—a familiar mixture of Georgian and later brick, weather-boarding, plaster and colour-wash. In Nos. 4–6 were born the Westall brothers—both book illustrators of the Regency. Richard did the 'English Classics', William topographical tours. West Street was once part of the B road to Essendon—now diverted past County Hall. There is a footpath across water meadows to *Hertingfordbury*. *Balls Park* (now a college) is reputed to date from c. 1640, but looks more Queen Anne, or early Georgian, than anything else—that is until one recalls the similar details of *Tyttenhanger*. Its architect was Peter Mills, who must have been as ahead of his time as Inigo Jones was—a puzzling house.

Hertingfordbury [5] Huge parish of mild hills and water-meadows between Hertford and Welwyn. The bypassed village has a bridge

over the Mimram, a short main street with Georgian-fronted *White Horse* inn, mellow 17th- and 18th-century houses, and a 19th-century church in a leafy setting near by. Inside the last are some Jacobean and Georgian *monuments*, including one by Roubiliac. The giant, idiosyncratic Gothick *Panshanger* is now gone, but the landscaped grounds by Repton, with the bloated, bridged Mimram as a picturesque centre-piece, remain virtually intact. Truly sublime. At *Cole Green* a special railway station was built for the mansion. At *Letty Green*, *Woolmer's Park*, on a hillside, has a long Doric colonnade and a sweeping lime avenue.

Hexton [2] A thin Hertfordshire peninsula crammed with more picturesque instances than the whole surrounding sea of Bedfordshire. Forget the chalk scuffed up in fields to the south and imagine limestone cottages in place of the mock Tudor estate versions or those of crumbling plaster and thatch. Gaze up at the encircling wooded hills and suddenly the Cotswolds are recalled. Banish this vision and one of Kent takes over. Hertfordshire seems miles away on the ramparts of *Ravensburgh Castle*, the vast (over 20 acres), oblong Iron Age hill fort high up on the tree-dotted *Barton Hills*. This is ideally sited on a plateau surrounded on three sides by steep combes. The main entrance is via a neck of land to the north-west. There is an encompassing single ditch and bank, while on the west side a double ditch marks the county boundary with Bedfordshire. Surely we stand in prime earthwork country—Wessex or Sussex! Down below smoke curls above roof-tops and misty gardens of apple trees in this unmistakably squirarchal community. As well as the sham timbering, past residents of the ponderous mid-Victorian *Manor* have contributed the 1929 brick *Village Hall*, which looks like a cricket pavilion and once doubled

Balls Park, **Hertford**

as an impromptu cinema, and also the Gothic revival pump ('for the villagers') at the crossroads. The manor grounds, partly enclosed by a Colditz-style ivy-clad wall contains a long lake with bridges, elegant drives and a grove of box-trees. St Faith's *church* is an oddity in a damp setting with yews. Cement-faced, completely restored (date uncertain), but preserving stubby medieval arcading, tracery and corbels. When the tower collapsed in 1947 plate glass was inserted in the tower arch thus giving a peep-hole view of the ruins outside. Chancel is curtained across; east window glass is quasi Cubist. Minimalism, as applied to wall tablets in an example of 1601, features a central travertine panel.

High Cross [6] Ordinary main road community on a hillside overlooking Rib valley. Rough-hewn stone *church* of 1846 by Salvin, restorer of ancient castles and builder of a 'new' one at Peckforton in Cheshire, has a thin green spire and some odd stained glass by 'William Morris & Co.' influenced Selwyn Image (1893). Image, who was involved in the Aesthetic Movement, and in particular the Century Guild, was described as 'the last significant Pre-Raphaelite . . .' by Paul Nash. In a field at *Standon Green End* a railed boulder commemorates the landing of Lunardi, his dog, cat and a pigeon in September 1784, after the first balloon voyage made in England. They had taken off from Moorfields.

High Wych [6] (Wych pronounced to rhyme with High) A hectic flourishing of High Churchiness in an unlikely roadside setting. Outside: flint and brick with a bizarre little pencil tower. Inside: hushed and dim, but having an apse aflame with the ox-blood scribblings of some manic proto Art Nouveauish decorator working *c*.1861. At isolated *Allen's Green* a timbered

Christ's Hospital School for Girls, **Hertford** (*above*); **Hertford** Castle (*below*) ▷

Hinxworth

chapel has bottle-green glass, and looks strangely New Englandish.

Hinxworth [2] Hinxworth is to Bedfordshire what Puttenham is to Buckinghamshire. In their respective characters, and in the landscape they inhabit, both belong to their neighbouring counties. Hinxworth, with Newnham and Ashwell, is part of the East Bedfordshire/South Cambridgeshire plain. An open, undistinguished, straight village street in a landscape of wide, unhedged fields drained by ditch-like tributaries of minor rivers, of pylons, of wispy coppice-wood, and to the east Ashwell church tower playing the role of a Boston stump against a tall sky. *Church* (St Nicholas), of flint with dressings and tracery of Totternhoe stone, is now in the ideal

state of picturesque decay. How could Cotman or Prout have missed that leaning south porch, that leprous window tracery (far worse on the south side), that tower? A suitably friendly interior has whitened walls, pine pews, a rather good late 15th-century brass, a pair of elegant wall tablets by T. King, and biblical texts (local influence of Wesley showing?). In the main street a village clock at the top of a 30-ft stuccoed tower which also serves as war memorial. In Chapel Street two excellent timber-framed buildings face each other. One, *Cammocks*, is delightful. At the street-end a yew marks the site of the garden where once John Wesley walked. Across fields to the south *Hinxworth Place*, built of clunch from Ashwell quarry in 1460, preserves some original

features. The ghost of a monk haunts it.

Hitchin [2] Wealthy medieval borough on the River Hiz. F. L. Griggs, the etcher and book illustrator born here in 1876, called it 'one of the most beautiful small towns of England'. It had grown rich on wool-fulling and wool-trading, on vellum and parchment making, on tanning and rope weaving, and on a malting industry. It had markets for straw plait (made into hats in Luton) and corn. It had lavender fields in Griggs's time. Today Hitchin's medieval heart is essentially unchanged. Gloriously wide and airy Bancroft curves south into a narrower High Street which in turn enters a perfectly sized market square from which narrow Bucklersbury, Sun Street,

Hitchin

and lanes leading to the church and river, radiate. A very compact plan, with the southern end bounded by the town's finest medieval thoroughfare, Tilehouse Street, and its continuation, Bridge Street. Queen Street forms the eastern boundary. Everywhere are jagged rooflines of medieval or Tudor gables and orange tiles, gables of plaster or timber, many with deep overhangs and some obviously bricked over in Georgian times, good brick town houses for the wealthy, and handsome inns with generous carriageways. There are narrow alley-ways and curious back lanes. One lane off the Market

Place starts as a shopping arcade and finishes in a largish alcove used as an antique market on Saturdays. Hitchin is both conservative and cosmopolitan in a small town (population 29,000) way. In this most civilized of shopping towns there are morning coffee and antique shops and old-fashioned businesses as well as the High Street's chain stores and Churchgate's brash new shopping centre. An Asian quarter thrives off Nightingale Road. There is a dowdy-looking town-edge hospital, a tedious museum, and a broken-down cinema. But the old buildings are cherished, unlike those, say, of

Upper King Street, Royston, a less wealthy town. Hitchin's most uplifting sight is of the massive *church* lying alongside the new market's colourful tented (like a Bedouin encampment) stalls—a symbol of an historic town nicely in tune with the late 20th century. St Mary's has a squat tower as mighty as a castle gatehouse, a rich Perpendicular porch taller than a modern house and paid for by a merchant, a flint and brick-patched nave *riddled* with windows of Perpendicular tracery, buttresses stiffening out like wings, and battlements everywhere. Interior of light and space has Decorated

113

arcades which lead to a glorious mid-15th-century screen and contemporary chapels flanking an earlier chancel. All colour and incident crammed into this east end. South chapel floor is yellow with worn, late medieval brasses. Cluttering walls are all styles of mainly 18th-century Radcliffe monuments. Roof of stone and wooden angels. North chapel has table tombs in telling contrast. Crudely carved shields and quatrefoils as usual, but whereas two tombs are chalky and crumble the third has its stone front burnished to a fish belly pinky-greyness. Poppyheaded stalls in the chancel; the singular north aisle 'ceiling' of carved panels could be early 14th century; stone 15th-century pulpit. Individual notable buildings are too numerous to list, but a few stand out: Bancroft's late-17th-century *Skynner almshouses*, of dour brick; Sun Street's stately Georgian *Sun Inn*; Bridge Street's north side huddle of timber framing; Bucklersbury's *George Inn*, with its gaping coach carriageway; the Market Place's odd *Corn Exchange* of 1851, striking out among gentle Georgian façades; the *Priory*, incorporating arches and piers of Carmelite house, but parading an Adam south front which overlooks landscaped parkland reaching past suburbia to the riverside hamlet of *Charlton*, birthplace of Henry Bessemer, pioneer of cheap steel manufacture. The Churchyard's tiny old shops cluster in a horseshoe around the church. Near-by Aram's Alley and former baker's shop of F. L. Griggs's father are haunted. Tilehouse Street is a gem from end to end. Who can say how much medieval timber lies under the handsome Georgian brick fronts? Nos. 81–82 is one survival—15th century and possibly a guildhall. George Chapman, translator of Homer and hack playwright, was born at No. 35 in 1559. Homer's ghost summoned him on Hitchin Hill. Plaque. Artist Birkit Foster was also a Hitchin man. *Gosmore* is a

meadowy hamlet with a shaded main street of modest cottages and showier 18th-century brick. At *Oughton Head* one of Britain's shortest rivers (1¾ m.) springs from silvery mud to water a chalky cleft, beechwood-fringed, to Ickleford.

Hoddesdon [9] In medieval times Hoddesdon had a market (although no parish church until 1844) when Cheshunt and Broxbourne were ordinary small villages along the high road to London from Hertford and Cambridge. Today all three are joined (with others) by continuous brickwork. Hoddesdon's High Street becomes Broxbourne's High Road, and so on. Yet, despite attempts to wreck it by full-blooded road schemes, the place has managed to retain its small country-town character, mainly by virtue of its High Street. The delights begin here, at its south end, behind the Georgian *Lowewood* and neo-Georgian Council Offices. In *Follies and Grottoes* (1953) Barbara Jones writes about the Gothick bathhouse, buttery and orangery (among other things) created by Quaker builder John Warner in *c*. 1800 in the grounds of his *Woodlands*. Today, presumably in what remains of the estate, *Little Woodlands*, an eccentric yellow-brick house with a clock, and *The Orangery*, stucco, gilding, a colonnade with steps, lie together in a bosky hollow, bullied somewhat by Broxbourne Council's contribution to the scene of a disturbingly red *Civic Hall*. Apparently the Orangery owner would not sell. Behind the near-by offices stands the stone-carved *Samaritan Woman* given to the town as a conduit head in 1625. Prior remembered seeing it in the Market Place: 'Into an Old Inn did this Equipage roll,/At a Town they call Hodsdon, the Sign of the Bull,/Near a Nymph with an Urn, that divides the Highway,/And into a Puddle throws Mother of TEA.' (*Down-Hall*, a ballad—written in 1715) Prior's

High-way continues north with two mansions almost facing one another. *Rawdon House*, characteristically brick Jacobean with gables and central tall porch, is dated 1622 and was once a nunnery, now offices. A similar fate awaits the Georgian-fronted *Grange*. After this the High Street proper comes into view past the Elizabethan timbers of the *Golden Lion* inn. A wide and airy shopping street composed mainly of quiet (and even old-fashioned) shopfronts with cared-for mellow brick upper stories. Some timbering as in the row of cottages next to a strikingly Pickwickian coaching inn—*The White Swan*. On the opposite side, farther south, some good Georgian houses together. John McAdam, roadmaker extraordinary, lived at No. 68. The *Bull Inn* has long gone. Infilling is intelligently done and the one wholesale development does not dominate. The street is now pedestrianized half-way along. Hoddesdon's incubus happens also to be its greatest landmark. Heading the High Street, bullying the tiny Market Place, dwarfing the yellow 1835 clock-tower and drab red *church* of St Paul (18th-century gallery inside) is a nine-storey tower block, recognizably mid 'sixties and dated already, rising above a brash shopping precinct. It was built when the population was well under 20,000. Going north, between a pair of roundabouts, there are riding stables on the dual carriageway. East from here, past the terraces of *Rye Park*, over the railway and opposite a speedway track and waterside inn, stand the remains of the infamous *Rye House*. A mid 15th-century brick gatehouse preserving original features and surrounded by a moat. In 1683 the plan was to ambush the king as he returned to London from Newmarket via the misty *Rye Meads*. The royal plans were changed, the plotters betrayed and executions followed. The spot appears now to be a picnic area with brightly

114

coloured signs. Billowing acres of woodland west of the town's bypass.

Holwell [2] Dull chalk-belt village strung along an S-bend by Bedfordshire border. Church, rebuilt by Ewan Christian in 1877–9 using the old material, preserves Perpendicular features and a curious 1515 brass to Richard Wodehouse, a priest. Instead of heraldry, two 'wodewoses' or wild men—an innocent pun. Excellent neo-Tudor *almshouses* of 1832 and 1885 and *school* of 1841. Off the road to Shefford, by a disused railway, *Old Ramerick* has an imposing William and Mary front.

Hormead, Great [3] In a hollow formed by a partially culverted stream the main street features prosperous farmhouses and cottages, many with large frontages. Georgian-fronted *Dane End* farm, the Tudor *Old Rectory*, with its overhang and tall chimney-stacks, and the picturesquely positioned *Milburns*, are outstanding. Then, after the street opens out, the long, low, thatched *Cottage*, pierced by Gothick windows, its lemon-yellow plaster contrasting violently with a nightmarish cedar, is impossible to miss. It once featured in a TV advertisement for paint. A near-by footpath leads to St Nicholas's *church* via beech trees and the extraordinarily romantic *Great Hormead Bury*, which is Georgian and semi-derelict. *Church* was ruined by Blomfield in 1872–3, but retains a medieval tower, arcades and humorous corbels. Gargoyles are of a devil, a laughing monk, and a most benign lion. *Brick House* (1 m. NE.), enviably situated in trees along a farm lane, got its name from the time when bricks were scarce. Bastion-like, and with walls 4 feet thick in places, its mysteries include blocked slit windows and a cabbalistic '969' on a wall. A possible date is 1579. More romantic from a distance than close at hand.

Hormead, Little [3] On a bleak, treeless ridge above Great Hormead a lane of straggling cottages and farmhouses with an illustrious little *church* of St Mary alone in a field. Of flint with cement, the tiny Norman nave has north and south doors with a boisterous display of mouldings and an original window. A 13th-century chancel. A plain and simple, even Spartan, interior fit for a water-colourist, with dampness, lime and ancient worn-out timber. Beneath the eloquent nave roof-beams, possibly Norman, is a delicately chiselled Decorated font. Facing this the north door woodwork *is* Norman and is faced with the most masterly display of 12th-century ironwork in the country—scrolls, stylized flowers, birds, or perhaps a dragon. An endearing brick porch and a shingled towerlet.

Hunsdon [6] Its houses start where Widford's leave off. A straggling main street of white weather-boarding, plaster and brick has its share of modern development. Tiny green with Victorian pump. *Pump House* opposite conceals, under plaster, a medieval hall house. Facing this, an end cottage of long, curving range boasts two 4-ft-high carvings of ?Pegasus beneath its overhang. Towards Widford on the right *'The Original Turkey Cock Inn'* claims to be 'the world's most exclusive pub'. Past the ghost of an airfield, a lane winds down to *Hunsdon House* and *church* of St Dunstan. Looking east from the churchyard a sudden eyeful of brick and greenery and such queer shapes against the sky. Farthest away the plum-coloured box of the much-altered mansion that Henry VIII once rebuilt, its crenellations echoed by those on the pretty little gatehouse turret nearer us. Nearer still ?Victorian stables are built on to a crumbling churchyard wall. Over the wall the north *chapel*'s Tudor brick shades lush grass. And the shapes—the pinnacled stable ventilators, stern and business-like,

the tiny adjacent tower with its shingled, pointed roof and bull weather-vane, the turret's brick corbel table, the churchyard tomb overrun by saplings and exotic-looking invaders from over the wall. More Tudor brick around corner in the south chapel. A timber porch, as massive as a lych-gate is bold against the flint and rendering that composes the rest of the church. A drab, disappointing interior is redeemed by high-quality furnishings that befit close association with two large estates (the other is *Briggens*, 1 m. SSW.). A glorious Jacobean oak screen is the best of its date in Hertfordshire—fluted pilasters, slim columns, a vivacious strapwork affair, and a crowning cornice on which two horses' heads, one black, one white, glare. Above them a swan balances, wings poised. Contemporary family box pews and pulpit. *Monuments* are all excellent: two Jacobean examples to John Carey and wife and Thomas Forster show effigies, the former featuring the same horses and swan as the screen, the latter heavily railed around. A recessed brass to Francis Poyntz (d. 1528) is surrounded by Perpendicular stonework that seems oddly old hat for the date. A most curious memorial is to James Gray, 'Parke and Hous-Keper' (d. 1591) at Hunsdon. Etched on brass is skeletal Death stabbing Gray as the hunter aims at a stag—the sort of grim irony so relished by the Elizabethans and their forebears. Bright glass of saints and angels together with tracery remain from the mid 15th-century building. *Briggens*, majestic in its rolling parkland of ornamental pools, is partly early Georgian, and is best seen from the train on the railway below. Roadside farmhouse near entrance has Gothick windows.

Ickleford [2] River Oughton's trees screen it from suburban Hitchin, to little effect. New estates have already crossed over and spoilt a

Ickleford

land of St Ibbs, a favourite haunt of F. L. Griggs, Hitchin's great etcher and book illustrator. It has lakes and a stone bridge. On the roadside towards Langley is a group of quirky Gothick thatched cottages dwarfed by beeches.

Kelshall [3] Like neighbours Therfield and Reed, a parish on the chalk ridge that hangs over the Bedfordshire/Cambridgeshire plain. A district of plunging prairie fields and isolated farmsteads to the north, with coppices and clay ponds to the south. Village is a windswept settlement in lost lanes. *Church* (St Faith) is hidden among trees between farm barns and rambling Georgian *Rectory*. It is restored (1870) Perpendicular, with a harmonious interior that features two curiosities: a 12-ft-high niche in the north-west corner of the north aisle that is roomy enough for two people and was probably a home for a processional cross and banners; and four ghostly images of saints in faded red and gold, and in the dress of *c.* 1400, painted on the chancel screen panels. Lower part of the churchyard cross is now used as sundial. In *Philpott's Wood* (1 m. S.) the mound site of ancient *Wood Hall* has a damp, highly romantic setting. Alas, no fabric remains.

pleasant straggling main street. Close by are pub, shop, and roadside stabling (clock dated 1819) of the big house. St Katherine's *church* crouches stuccoed behind cedars. The icing may have arrived with Giles Gilbert Scott's south aisle, chapel, and vestry, in 1859. His sugar-candy mouldings are pastiches that beg applause. Compare them with the real thing, the joyous zig-zags around the Norman south door and blocked north door. A reverent, rather 'High' church odour. Fierce Green Man on corbel.

Ippollitts [2, 5] (St Ippollitts) Intriguing name of an unspecial

hilltop village, directly south of Hitchin's red-roofed sprawl. On the brow a miniature green, neo-Tudor school, former inn with close-set timbers and overhang, all primly painted, and *church* of St Ippolyts, dedicated to a third-century martyr and horse doctor. Structure dates from 11th century onwards, but was rebuilt skilfully in the 1870s using the old materials. Some lively stonework inside: life-like corbel masks of monk, bishop, nun, lady and man with odd headgear; priest effigy in recess; and another looking like John Stuart Mill, but isn't. Perpendicular north porch is unused. Churchyard looks on to cool-leaved park-

Kimpton [5] In rolling country a riverless valley ends with this main-street village of red late-Victorian villas and earlier plain brick cottages. At the prettier east end a lane climbs to The Green, an oddly positioned square of turf surrounded by cottages, and the *church* of St Peter and St Paul. This is visually uninspiring from the outside, like many a plain, much restored Perpendicular church, but inside is a different story. Nave arcades of pointed arches and round piers having scalloped and floriate capitals are patently Transitional. Bloxam's category of 'semi-Norman' perfectly describes the stone-carving. There is a de luxe

117

Breachwood Green mill, **King's Walden**

Perpendicular arcade in the chancel which also contains dull contemporary screens and poppy-headed stalls.

Kings Langley [7] Gadeside commuter village that wears its vital place in history lightly, almost imperceptibly. Of the *royal palace* where Edmund de Langley, England's first Duke of York and great-grandfather of the man who led the White Rose faction, was born little remains. A wine cellar was discovered under a school gym, a half-mile west of the parish church. Of the Decorated church where Edmund's tomb stood until the Dissolution only a bit of wall remains. But of the contemporary Dominican *Priory* where the absurd Piers Gaveston was buried after his execution in 1314 a two-storey building, once an ivy-covered ruin, but now repaired and part of the school, can be seen. Strung out on the ridge below, the High Street tries to shake off the influence of Hemel and Watford and become recognizably villagey. It starts off well with a chequer brick *Rose and Crown* and its Regency verandah; then converted brick cottages and two larger Georgian houses belonging to a dentist and a garage. Very Home Counties demeanour. *Church* is broad, spread out, and of an entirely Perpendicular character, if not origin, with wide aisles and chancel chapels and pews flooding up into the tower. Poor Victorian stained glass fills every window, but those in the clerestory. The canopied pulpit is Jacobean and, with its carvings of ?dragons everywhere, must be one of Hertfordshire's finest. The carved heraldry on Edmund de Langley's tomb-chest (of *c.* 1402 and repainted) effectively echoes the more accomplished lozenge design on a chest of 1528 opposite. A patch of faded encaustic tiles on the floor. Average Tudor brasses.

King's Walden [5] Parish of switchback scenery on a Chiltern spur. The hills are patched with woods, and nearer the tiny village, the hedge ditches are bright with

King's Walden

comfrey and holly hedges sculpted into miniature tree-forms. A calm broken by an occasional boom from Luton airport. Church overlooks a placid world of yew hedges, trim lawns and exotic shubbery surrounding the spanking-new neo-Georgian pile that replaced a heavy late Victorian mansion on the site of an Elizabethan manor. Beyond the formal grounds a romantic parkland of giant oaks circled by nettles extends eastwards and ends in lodges. Peculiarly gloomy lime-tree avenue to house. *Church* is a contrast in styles, inside and out: mortar-caked and weather-beaten Perpendicular tower on a Victorian flint nave and chancel; an orange and purplish brick mid 17th-century vestry having wooden 'Gothic' window tracery and looking disconcertingly like a Victorian schoolroom. A brightly-lit nave featuring Early English arcades with robustly carved scroll, fleur-de-lis, cartouche and scalloped

capitals. A gaudy chancel where the floor tiles colour-match the fair-ground blues and reds on a 15th-century screen. The Victorian stone pulpit effectively mixes naturalism with late Gothicism. In a dour Baptist *chapel* at *Breachwood Green* is a 1658 pulpit from which John Bunyan preached.

Knebworth [5] Old and new Knebworth; Lytton and Lutyens. Modern Knebworth, with the population of a small town, grew up quickly around the station from *c.* 1905. It has prosperous houses, modest shops, *churches* (including a startling affair by Lutyens in *St Martin*) and a golf *clubhouse* of 1908, also by Lutyens, who designed cottages in Deard's End Lane and Park Lane. In the station's new subway is a huge and venerable grapevine luckily saved from destruction. Commuters share the fruit harvest. *Old Knebworth* lies scattered in pretty lanes on the edge

of the parkland that reflects the tastes and romantic temperament of its one-time owner, Lord Bulwer Lytton, an absurd and unreadable Victorian novelist and 'poet'. Of this landscape he wrote in 1835: '. . . its venerable avenues, which slope from the house down to the declivity of the park, giving wide views of the opposite hills, crowded with cottages and spires, impart to the scene that peculiarly English, half stately and wholly cultivated, character . . .' A well-observed sketch. He goes on to mention the church, *Grecian mausoleum*, browsing deer, and the small, picturesque fishing cottage on the lake. Very little has changed. Massive Newton Wood blocks out a certain view of Stevenage's industrial quarter and is also the perfect backdrop for the miniaturized pastoralism. The house is a Regency 'Tudor' confection, E-shaped, caked in icing-sugar stucco, and bristling with fake details. In *banqueting hall*,

119

△ **Knebworth**: Lytton Lytton by Thomas Green, 1710

William Lytton by Edward Stanton, 1705 ▷

dating from 1492, is some lavish oak and pine panelling and a rich Jacobean screen. Library is interesting. Elsewhere it is difficult to escape from Lytton—his image, his memorabilia, his taste for full-blooded High Victorian Gothic (best seen in his study). In the 'Chinese' (wallpapered) bedroom Dickens got the idea of the dog Gyp's pagoda. Other visitors included the painter Egg, the *Punch* editor Lemon, and John Leech. Mainly Norman and 15th-century *church* of St Mary and St Thomas still moves the imagination. Grey on a green hillock; shaded by moping trees; and engulfed by wide parkland. Lytton chapel, rebuilt in 1705, is stuffed with family *monuments* of the finest quality—three effigies of boldest Queen Anne Baroque, some Tudor brasses. In the chancel look for the 1662 epitaph and bust to Judith Strode.

Langley [5] Bungalows, cottages and a diamond-paned chapel litter a lane sloping down to the *Farmer's Boy* inn. Stevenage's shimmering skyline appears on the horizon. In a motor-car scrapyard at *Rush Green* nettles pierce the sockets in rusting skulls. From *Shilley Green* a lane tunnels through leaves patched with sunlight, twisting and dipping towards the cool glades of Hitch Wood.

Lemsford [5] Tucked away on a river-side lane between Welwyn Garden City and Brocket Park. Cottages, water-mill, waterfall and, near the main road, two engaging Georgian brick lodges flanking the big drive. Rock-faced *church* of 1859 has very earnest reproduction Perpendicular chapel of 1930 attached. *Brocket Hall* (unfortunately not open to the public), once the home of Lord Palmerston, Lord Melbourne, and his fatuous wife, Lady Caroline Lamb, 'friend' of Lord Byron, is an austere, rather boxish mansion, finished *c.* 1775, and best viewed from the end of its overgrown

Sir Edwin Lutyens at **Knebworth**: (*this page*) St Martin; (*opposite*) Homewood

Knebworth

avenue, by rusting roadside ironwork. Long, snaking lake created out of the Lea has obligatory balustraded stone bridge. Saloon ceiling is decorated with paintings begun by John Hamilton Mortimer (1741–79), proto-Romantic painter of the grotesque and horrible, dissolute, and a cricketer. Many footpaths through the wooded grounds.

Letchworth [2] Tiny village swept into the Garden City master plan but left on a limb in the far south-west corner, bowered in trees. *Hall*, now (of course) a hotel, is of Jacobean brick and has many gables, leaded windows, and, inside, a contemporary screen. St Mary's *church*, small and unpretentious, contains a door with 13th-century iron hinges, some 15th-century benches and a tiny ?early 14th-century stone effigy of a knight holding his heart in his hands–grisly.

Letchworth Garden City [2] Still there are the tile-hung and pebble-dashed nooks of the middle-class, vegetarian teetotallers who flocked to Ebenezer Howard's social experiment in its early days. But fast dying off are these

Old Letchworth Types whom Betjeman wickedly caricatured in 'Group Life: Letchworth'. Folksongs, handicrafts, an invigorating stroll on the Common with a cup of cheering Bovril to follow? Hardly likely nowadays. The pubs arrived in the 'sixties and wholefood is no longer a joke. The cosy homesteads, steep gables, white verandahs, silver birches and all, are snapped up as expensive period pieces, while down on the City's southern boundary bleak overspill estates house the New Letchworth Types. And not a boulevard or clipped lawn to be seen. Yet Letchworth remains the first of its kind in the world, a legend and an inspiration. In *Garden Cities of Tomorrow*, a revised version of his pioneering *Tomorrow: a Peaceful Path to Real Reform*, Howard, a social idealist concerned about rural depopulation and urban squalor, defined a garden city as a 'town-country magnet' uniting in one place the best of both worlds: high wages, low rents, clean air, social amenities, sound housing, etc. Industry, housing and shops were to be zoned and the whole surrounded by a purely agricultural belt. Interest was shown, money

raised and sites looked at. Finally, in 1903, 3,800 acres of fields and common land between three tiny villages were bought. Architect/planners Barry Parker and Raymond Unwin were hired and building began. Early on faddism and dottiness coexisted with architectural pragmatism. Down Nevells Road the *Skittles Inn* (1907), since converted, looked the picture of a country pub, but served lemonade and ginger beer only. Facing are some '*cheap cottages*' from the 1905 Exhibition designed to demonstrate minimal cost mass-housing for agricultural and industrial workers, the selling price being around £150. More of these in Quadrant, Icknield Way and Wilbury Road; much concrete and steel were used. Then there was an Urban Cottage Exhibition centred on Lytton Avenue. Same wholesome plainness. But there was also the *Cloisters*, built 1906–7 as a school for theosophical meditation by Cowlishaw, and one of Britain's craziest architectural fantasies. Looking partially composed from the odd bits and pieces of a Garden City builder's yard, it is nevertheless startlingly original in its use of traditional materials and decora-

Brocket Hall, **Lemsford** ▷

Letchworth Garden City

tive motifs. Casual callers unwelcome. Letchworth's chief glory, however, are the large detached houses in big grounds built along grand boulevards such as Sollershott West, East, and the Broadway; and also along the Hitchin and Baldock roads; and in Letchworth lane. Eminent and not so eminent architects are represented here as elsewhere: Baillie Scott, Crickmer, Riccardo (an unsuccessful competitor for the master plan), and Parker and Unwin themselves. The style was broadly vernacular (what else, given Howard's principles?) enlivened by much Arts and Crafts theory and some originality. In Norton Way South, Parker's own house and studio, now a *museum* devoted to the Garden City, is an unashamedly rustic retreat of thatch and plaster, built 1907. Inside, the sitting-room shows the architect's strong Arts and Crafts sympathies; also, solemnly documented, is a definitive collection of Garden City memorabilia. From here turn up Hillshott, then Ridge Avenue and Ridge Road to appreciate what Parker, Unwin and others achieved in the way of villagey groupings of terraces (1906 and 1911) for humbler citizens. Directly south, off Pixmore Way, St Paul's *church* is a frowzy barn of flint and brick begun in c. 1923 but left unfinished. It was to have a great tower, chapel, and south aisle, but the money ran out. Letchworth town centre is a mild shock after the bosky suburbs. It is bitty. A diet of neo-Georgianism, as at Welwyn, fills in where shopping parades of the early type (a date 1909) seen in Station Road and Leys Avenue should have been built. The new shopping centre might suit a Midlands city, but certainly not a Garden City. Adjoining, *Palace Cinema* (1909) was one of the earliest purpose-built cinemas in England. Yet Broadway, a boulevard of Lombardy poplars which zings south-west–north-east to the Town Square, then the station, never got the civic showpieces that were planned in the balmy early days. *Museum/art gallery, library* and *Town Hall* are merely pompousty municipal. Much more exciting is the *Spirella corset factory*, a landmark by railway, which looks decidedly like an Arts and Crafts mansion.

Lilley [5] Village in austere, open but wooded country that recalls Shropshire. There are neo-Elizabethan and later estate cottages bearing the Docwra crest; a Georgian inn; and the sober Victorian *church* of St Peter. This was built by Thomas Jekyll, who also designed the woodwork for Whistler's 'Peacock Room'— although there is little to connect the two enterprises. Original fea-

126

tures incorporated into the 1871 structure include: Norman chancel arch; Perpendicular font; and lavish Docwra *monuments*. Among Lilley worthies were James Janeway, a dotty divine who wrote pious children's books in the 17th-century, and John Kellerman, an early 19th-century 'alchemist' discovered by Radical publisher Sir Richard Phillips in 1828, (see *A Personal Tour through the United Kingdom*).

Little Amwell *see* Amwell, Little

Little Berkhamstead *see* Berkhamstead, Little

Little Gaddesden *see* Gaddesden, Little

Little Hadham *see* Hadham, Little

Little Hormead *see* Hormead, Little

Little Munden *see* Munden, Little

Little Wymondley *see* Wymondley, Little

London Colney [8] Aptly named. Arid streets of bungalows, semis and shopping parades in a featureless landscape. By the stream-like Colne is a very early Norman revival roadside *church* of 1825. In this district of big hospitals, *Napsbury*, its buildings laid out among trees and flower-beds, is the most attractive. The Catholic *All Saints Pastoral Centre* was built in 1899 as an Anglican convent by Leonard Stokes, who also designed telephone exchanges. The impressive long front has a central gatehouse and cloisters behind and is of purplish-red brick lightened with orangey brick bands and relieved by Tudoresque mullioned windows. A lumbering pile having details of some flair. Comper's *chapel* of 1927 must be viewed from the south, where it rises from the water-meadows like a pale after-image of Eton's masterpiece. Or is it

Letchworth Garden City

All Saints Pastoral Centre, **London Colney**

Lancing? In the whitened interior there are cliffs of oak choir stalls between a blazing rose window and a vast Tree of Jesse that takes up most of the east wall. The altar under its golden baldachin, a touch of the Italian, is Comper's signature on his work. All this in the age of Gertrude Stein, quantum mechanics and Cubism!

Long Marston [4] Straggling crossroads place stuck in the dullish, well-watered flatlands north of Tring. The ruined, ivy-covered flint tower is all that remains of a deserted medieval church—a must for the modern-day follower of the *Tours of Dr Syntax* (Rowlandson). A new *church*, uninspired in itself, incorporates fragments of the old—chancel arch and windows—and also Perpendicular aisle piers from *Tring* parish church. In the main street are plain cottages, a bit of timber-framing, and weather-boarding in good

harmony. Some thoughtless new development. In 1751 the village *pond* was the scene of England's last witch-lynching when Ruth Osborn, the 'witch', was captured and drowned. One of her tormentors ended up gibbeted at *Gubblecote Cross* ($\frac{1}{2}$ m. E.), close to the moated site of a deserted medieval village.

Mackerye End [5] At one time spelt 'Mackarel End' according to Charles Lamb, who placed the Tudor and Jacobean (a front dated 1665) 'farmhouse' firmly on the literary pilgrim's map when he described a nostalgic visit to this childhood haunt in one of his best essays. Sited on a hilltop overlooking Harpenden's suburb of *Batford*.

Markyate [4] (or Markyate Street and Market Street). An old coaching stop on the Roman Watling Street and in the robust country south-west of Luton. Before the

1957 arrival of the bypass the narrow street of mainly plain brick cottages with carriageway arches was 'uninhabitable—a day and night stream of lorries travelling both ways' (Ian Nairn). More peaceful now, but quietly thriving with commuter estates on the western side. Strikingly positioned at the village head and behind trees is the Georgian *church* (Market Street was part of *Caddington* parish until this time) of St John the Baptist. There is a chequered brick tower and a nave of 1734, but it is otherwise unremarkable. The neo-Jacobean *Markyate Cell* looks period from a distance, and indeed incorporates bits from the mansion built in 1539–40 on the site of a Benedictine nunnery. Katherine Fanshawe, née Ferrers, of Markyate Cell, was very likely the fearless highway-person who terrorized travellers from early in 1660 until her death, aged 26, in June of that year. Her ghost haunts the Cell.

Meesden [3] On a windy ridge close to the Essex border. Wide verges then a rough, rudimentary village green around which are strung thatch and colour-wash, council homes, a water tower and a village hall. Concealed at the end of a woodland track off the lane to Langley is the *church* of St Mary. Screened from the former *Rectory* of 1695, it is an ordinary medieval building remarkable for two features—its porch and its floor mosaic. The former, built around 1530, is secular in spirit despite its Gothic endeavours, its windows, corbel table, buttresses et al. Inside the porch, vermilion brick colour creeps through the rendering like ochre markings in caves. Before the altar, the tiles forming a radiating pattern bordered by circles and quatrefoils, etc., in glazed blacks and yellows (and reds?) are early 14th century and stunning. Across the fields, Meesdenbury, a working farm, is partially moated.

Minsden [5] Ruins of a *chapel* which once served the parishes of *Langley* and *Preston*, and which, though derelict from the 17th century, was used for marriages until 1814. The broken outline of a 14th-century nave and chancel, shadowed by gesturing dead elms, and invaded by elder and nettles, stands on a hill. In summer the pointed arches and gables are sharp grey against sky-blue. Winter brings a terrible melancholy. Rumours of haunting abound—a ghostly Pan, a tolling bell. . . . In 1908 a spectral monk was captured on film. Hine, the Hertfordshire historian, had his ashes scattered here.

Moor Park [7] Arguably Britain's most palatial clubhouse. From an open road winding between birch, dells of bracken and fly agarics, with golf balls whirring white against the acid-green humps of hills, a magnificent grey apparition rounds into view. A wealthy South Seas merchant, Benjamin Styles, bought the whole estate in 1720 and set about, with Thornhill as architect, and then perhaps Leoni, remodelling a 17th-century house. Today we see a tall oblong box of Portland stone pierced with most French-looking windows and fronted by a gigantic, severely classical portico, reaching up to the roofline. Much rich rococo work inside and out, mainly the work of continental interior decorators. The full-blooded entrance hall, crammed with every embellishment, must be seen. The ballroom is by Adam and the park was remodelled by Capability Brown.

Much Hadham *see* Hadham, Much

Munden, Great [6] Also known as Much Munden. Paradoxically Great is smaller than Little. Parish population is confined to scattered

Mackerye End

farms and small communities of which *Nasty* (q.v.) is the largest. Parish of open upland is part of a band of cold and comfortless landscape running from Throcking down to Collier's End. No wonder medieval peasants abandoned their settlements here for the sheltered valleys below. There is a string of six known village sites in this belt alone. One is opposite Great Munden church, another lies at *Libury* (½ m. SE.). St Nicholas' *church* stands on rising ground in a churchyard of cutting winds. *Mundenbury* (1702), most recent structure of many on this site, stands behind. Going west there are only farms between here and the hamlet of Wood End, 2½ miles away. A church of Norman origin—see blocked north doorway and chancel north window—but much altered and restored has a tower with spike. Pudding-stone

was used in the foundations. Inside is a chapel-like gloom despite clear glass and a high, wide nave. Some quality 15th-century stonework includes exuberant ogees of tomb recesses, reredos niches and castellations. The pulpit was supposedly made in memory of Robert Cecil. One of the spacious choir stalls bears the insignia RK (?Robert King, Rector 1510–38)—a useful aid to dating. Two 17th-century rectors were Lady Margaret Professors of Divinity at Cambridge. At Plough Inn (⅔ m. S.) a theatre organ removed from the Gaumont, Finchley, is claimed to be the only one of its kind in a pub in the world. Attracts busloads at weekends.

Munden, Little [6] Larger in population than Great Munden, but smaller in area. A parish of bare upland and tiny communities on

lonely lanes. The largest settlement is at *Dane End* where recent private development and older council housing has swollen a handful of streamside cottages into a smallish village. On the hill to the north All Saints' *church* stands in an open churchyard near the *rectory* and a minute school of 1825. A church of elusive charm, bright and limewashed. The pine-pewed nave is dominated by an organ on a light-oak gallery reached by a whorl of steps. Perfect proportions. Cheerful herringbone and roll decoration on the capitals of the only remaining Norman work in the north aisle arcade—rest is 14th century. Other delights of this period are three engaging statuette niches in the nave wall and chancel tomb effigies to Sir John and Lady Thornbury, smothered with graffiti. The adjoining tombs to

130

Meesden

Philip and Margaret Thornbury are 15th century. On hydrocephalic figures, armour, costume and jewellery of lapidary ostentation, while above them swaggering ogees teem with crockets. Such richness.

Mymms, North [8]

The unsubtle A1(M) gashes this parish of woodland and big parks and commuter suburbs (like Welham Green) the size of small towns. In the streamside hamlet of *Water End* roses grow over the trellis letters of the former inn's 'garden' and there are transport cafés beached by the new motorway. There is no real village. St Mary's *church* lies close to the park edge, near cottages and the vicarage, but it and its own churchyard seem totally absorbed into the surrounding parkland. Built on characteristic late Decorated lines (nice tracery), but the tower, although with a battered door and window of this date, is said to be mid 15th-century. The spacious interior is gummed up by ubiquitous Victorian oak; bold corbels. Two notable brasses (both remounted) show a 15th-century knight simply, effortlessly incised, and a North Mymms vicar of *c*.1360 robed in vestments and standing in a niche that has a surround recalling the High Gothic richness of a cathedral's west front. Small and said to be Flemish. Adjoining is a large marble *monument* to Lord Somers, Chancellor in William III's reign. Above a functioning marble door a female figure of Justice holds scales. Most charming memorial is in the nave—a life-sized image of a flowery-dressed Elizabethan lady at prayer, realized in yards of ?bitumen-filled grooves in stone. There is a similar affair at *Watton-at-stone*. Churchyard has a yew-hedge path and views of elaborate black ironwork under lime-trees. *North Mymms House*, a minor Hatfield House but with major Victorian additions, hides effectively behind foliage. Visitors are not encouraged.

Mymms, South [8]

With Potters Bar it was transferred from Middlesex in 1965 and like Harefield (now in Greater London) retains the jaunty air of an old Middlesex village. There is a row of creeper-covered brick cottages and a Regency villa facing a tiny green, an old-fashioned post office and Victorian *almshouses*—all in a quiet island between three major roads and a gigantic motorway intersection. Contemporary neo-Georgian and 'twenties half-timber mingle on the road to Ridge. Red London buses turn around at the sanatorium. The largely Perpendicular *church* of St Giles had, in the age of Gilpin, a 'very picturesque' ivy-mantled tower. The ivy was probably removed in Victorian times when G. E. Street rebricked the north aisle, added rood screen, pulpit and lectern, and High Anglican decorators got to work with paint and gilding. The earlier glories are all from the 1520s and are the gift of Henry Frowyk, a wealthy London merchant: the panels of deep blue and purple glass depicting families at prayer, a convention taken from brasses; the brilliant openwork screens which cage the chancel and chapel; and the chapel itself. There are Frowyk *monuments*: chancel one has a canopy supported on a bulbous Elizabethan four-poster or refectory table balusters; chapel affair is old-fashioned Perpendicular and has a stone effigy carved with more craftsmanship than flair. Some strange wall tablets: in the nave a chalky outgrowth from a marble tablet features a tiny skull fronting a deep recess, like an eerie cave guardian; in the north aisle an inscription, distorted as if by water, is bordered by alien plant forms and a winged skull. At the bottom of the graveyard stands a po-faced 'Doric' *mausoleum*. A part-Georgian part-1929 vicarage adjoins. From Seven Dials to a house at *Dancer's Hill* James Catnach retired in 1838. He was the most celebrated (and wealthiest) penny-ballad and broadsheet seller of all time. Under *Mymmshall* woods are the ditches and mound of a Norman *castle*. Legend tells of treasure hidden at the bottom of a well north-east of 'Camlet' moat. Fields of *fritillaries* were once a common sight in South Mymms.

Nasty [6]

Belies its name, which is a corruption of nast-hyde. A tiny hamlet of Great Munden with a green tin *chapel* and old cottages on a lane that dips and then climbs into a wide sky.

Nettleden [4]

Tiny, secret place of mainly 17th-century cottages deep in a wooded crease of the Chilterns. Hellebore and bryony flourish in the shade of St Lawrence's nave and 1811 brick chancel. In a churchyard of sombre yews and fungi are two pudding-stone 'markers' and a moss-lined stone coffin. Past lattice-paned *Church House* narrow Spooky Lane (unsuitable for motors) eventually reaches Frithsden by slicing its way through the hill by means of a sheer-sided cutting which was flint and brick-faced by the Duke of Bridgewater's men in the early 19th century. A brick bridge carrying the now seedy avenue across to Ashridge was also their work. Spiralling slowly upwards from daylight to forest darkness, then back into sunshine, is a disturbing, dreamlike experience. At *Frithsden* (pronounced Freeze-den) hamlet a mock-Tudor oddity dated 1879 is girdled by technicolour marigolds. Near by stands a demure, white *chapel* of 1835. The Green has a beechwood backdrop. District was once celebrated for its black cherries—a fair being held here in high summer.

Newnham [2]

Down the hill from Caldecote and of a very different character. A shady streamside place with few pretensions and some charm. There are thatched properties along the Ashwell road, but the grandest house is of

Way to the church, **Meesden**

Georgian brick and faces the *church*. This is smothered in rosy cement and appears to be Regency Gothick. Inside, however, are early Perpendicular details, including a glorious font and a whole north nave wall covered with wall paintings discovered in 1963. A cloaked St Christopher paddles across a stream filled with most medieval-looking fish. Handsome *monuments*. Village has been without a pub since at least 1900.

Northaw [8] With church, pub, green and general stores this is surely a real English village. Look again. The church is late Victorian, rock-faced and East-Midlandish. The green is now a traffic island.

Many of the showier modern homes have carports and burglar alarms. Workaday, getting-and-spending London has rubbed its back against all but the grand gentlemen's residences scattered in the parkland around. *Northaw House*, once a hospital, now full of globe lampshades and architects, is white-painted William and Mary in scruffy grounds with chequered brick stables. Almost opposite, *Northaw Place*, so altered as to be unrecognizably 1690 in origin, has a lodge, lake, cedar and laurels. Near-by mid-Georgian *Dower House* has a chastening towny mien—like the old *Vicarage* back in the village. Can Hampstead be far off? To the south, off a woodland track now

made impassable by the jodhpur brigade, *The Hook* (avant garde for its 1839 date) is buried tantalizingly among greyhound kennels. Rhododendroned *lodge*.

Northchurch [7] Once more important than Berkhamsted, but now almost its suburb. River, canal, railway and the fumy A11 run together through a Chiltern cleft. To the north there is open common below *Ashridge* woods; to the south *Grims Ditch* threads its way through patchy coppice and plantation. Main-road village has a sprinkling of timber-framing (*Church House* is striking) and Georgian brick. St Mary's *church* has a 15th-century crossing tower, bits of

Tunnel and cutting, **Nettleden**

Saxon walling, and a brilliantly wrought continental chest, but is otherwise rather dull. Peter the 'wild-boy', an 18th-century German freak who ate grass and walked on all fours, was buried in the *churchyard*.

North Mymms *see* Mymms, North

Norton [2] With Willian and Old Letchworth was left virtually untouched in the agricultural belt encircling the world's first Garden City—no doubt as a model of instruction for new citizens on what

was good and bad about the traditional English village. Letchworth pilfered its *Common* and developments occurred only in the south of the parish, away from the old centre of church, early Victorian vicarage, and sprinkling of cottages in and around Church Lane. St Nicholas' *church*, Perpendicular with brick chancel of 1814, has a whitened interior, faded old red floor-tiles, a 17th-century canopied pulpit, a grandly simple Norman chancel arch, and two excellent Jacobean wall tablets. In all a gracious contrast of shape, colour and texture. Modest perfection.

Nuthampstead [3] Scattered civil parish (i.e. with no church) in hilly, open country east of Barkway. Moorland roads, a narrow corkscrew route to Anstey, patches of gleaming white weatherboarding and thatch. The airfield, recently rejected as a site for London's third airport, was an important American bomber base in the last war. Surrounding district has been the scene of many accidents, dangerous horseplay, and near escapes. Bits of the old runway were used as motorway rubble. Surviving sections are weed choked and melancholy. Post-war

South of **Northchurch**

bungalows line the main approach road. In 1946 a rare, possibly early 13th century, ivory *pendant* of Virgin and Child was found on a moated site in *Scales Park*, now conifer-thick, to the south.

Offley (or **Great Offley**) [5] Hilltop crossroads village on the strange Chiltern spur of frowning contours that eventually melt smilingly northwards into the Bedfordshire plain. A place recently spoilt by a mini housing estate in fields immediately opposite urbane *Offley Place* (by Smirke) and the Gothicized *church*. The comely brick cottages, timbered houses and pretty inns fail to compensate. However, the churchyard mulberry-tree is a good sign. St Mary Magdalene is unashamedly a hybrid. The nave is medieval (13th century), the tower 1800, the chancel a Gothick remodelling of 1777 by Thomas Salusbury, uncle of Dr Johnson's Mrs Thrale. This last is faced with Portland stone, raised above nave height (an odd sight) and equipped with toy-fort crenellations and funny corner pinnacles. Inside the nave the floriated arcades lean dangerously out of true. Ahead, the chancel beckons enticingly, curtained off like an inner sanctum, sumptuous with marble memorials, with fiddly rococo plasterwork and a tent-like canopy over the east

window, with choirboy corbels, and with busts in niches. All lit from above by roof lantern. Showpiece monument by Nollekens depicts Sir Thomas and wife classically attired before a sturdy, sash-draped dwarf oak, its bark crazed and fissured in most clayey marble. Other good *monuments*, but they are pedestrian in comparison. Excellent font panels each carved with different 14th-century tracery. *Little Offley* (1½ m. N.) is a lonely late-Tudor brick manor at a lane's end.

Oxhey [8] Semi-rural suburb of Watford until the post-war housing estates began filling in much open space towards the old Middlesex (now Greater London) boundary. Some of *Oxhey Wood* was spared, but not the grounds of *Oxhey Place* where the surviving brick-and-flint *chapel* of 1612 (repaired and restored by the Victorians) once stood near farm buildings. Chapel interior is dignified by oak reredos and other woodwork of 1690, and a wall monument to chapel builder, James Altham.

Pirton [2] Large rambling place on the edge of the Bedfordshire plain. The view towards the church from where the High Street curves with terraced cottages by a duckpond—the sight of raw modern

housing filling gaps between the old village lanes—is pure South Bedfordshire. Older buildings are generally loners in their own good cultivating soil; groupings are rare. Pirton is best seen from the huge central pasture-like open space, which was once part of a Norman enclosed settlement, of which the partially-moated and distinctly scraggy *Toot Hill*, by the church, was the keep-mound. *Church* (St Mary) is also Norman—big, bluff, cruciform, and of flint faced with crazy-paving stone. After the tower collapsed in 1874, taking the transepts with it, the old materials were used in the rebuilding. But with the north transept not replaced the pile from a distance looks oddly like a castle gatehouse, or a semi-ruined priory church. Pure white light floods through a nave the size of a tithe barn. The spirit is Norman; the detail (windows, corbels, some stained glass) is Perpendicular; and there is no clutter. Pirton's big Jacobean farm and manor-houses have a fittingly honest and easy-going charm: timbered *Hammonds*; *Old Hall* (the date 1609 and more crazy-paving); stone *Rectory Farm* has barns and dovecot; *The Grange*, up against the Bedfordshire border near Shillington, is picturesquely moated and has a connecting bridgehouse of timber; *High Down*, by far the most exciting of the lot,

only slowly at first. From around 2,000 in 1908 the population has swollen to the present 25,000 in an explosion of speculative housing of all types—Edwardian 'nice modern villas' through Tudor bungalows, all sporting a peculiar porch, to 'sixties utility.

Preston [5] Well-preened, respectable place of large private houses; a terrace in Church Lane by Lutyens; a monolithic excrescence by the same architect on the original Queen Anne house of *Temple Dinsley* (now a girl's school surrounded by a mile of wall and fence); and the striking *church* of St Martin. This is boldly modern for its time (1900); a west elevation evokes a rocket ship, rectangular windows between token buttresses, a pebble-dashed exterior. And yet it inspired the antiquarian F. L. Griggs to an atmospheric drawing only months after its completion. There is a plainly functional nave, a conventionally Gothic chancel, and a collection of hassocks embroidered by villagers. In mood belonging more to a garden suburb or Metroland. Churchyard of cypresses. Dour Victorian *Castle Farm* replaces the 18th-century home of Captain Robert Hinde, the prototype of Sterne's Uncle Toby in *Tristram Shandy*. His humble farm was fitted with battlements, turrets, a portcullis and earthworks. On important occasions the eccentric Hinde would march into Hitchin at the head of suitably attired retainers. Preston is encircled by woodland. Bunyan often preached in a dell at *Wain Wood*, to the north.

lies under one of the beechwoods that crown the stupendous rolling chalkland to the south. The *Icknield Way* is scored white through buckthorn scrub hereabouts. *Money Knoll* is the burial place of an Ancient British chieftain. Three hollow taps heard mean he is making sure that his treasure chest is still there—according to legend.

Potten End [7] Dispersed, suburban Chiltern community with the cricketer Fred Titmus as its sub-postmaster.

Potters Bar [8] Removed from Middlesex in 1965, Potters Bar is

best viewed from the motorway where it rises from a sandy heath like a small Moorish city of brick and glass. Scant evidence of pottery manufacture. The medieval Le Pottere family lived near by and there is a house named Potterells in North Mymms. 'Bar' was probably a gate into Enfield Chase. By 1842 the tiny farming hamlet, turned Great North Road coaching stop, had a pious patent stone *church* (demolished), a Baptist *chapel* and a National School as well as older inns (still there) and medieval *Wyllyots Manor* down countrified Darkes Lane. Residential growth followed the station's arrival, but

Puckeridge [6] A hamlet and twin of Standon. Its twisting High Street of timber-framed and modest Georgian houses, comfortable old inns and two banks gives it the character of a small town. The

Temple Dinsley, **Preston**

bypass diverted traffic, but unfortunately cut across an important Roman site.

Puttenham [4] Hertfordshire's farthest-west village is a trickle of dull, windblown buildings on a lost-looking lane going nowhere. There are tall sky and level views across the Aylesbury plain from St Mary's *church* shrouded in its churchyard trees. It has flint chequer-work of the 14th century, a 15th-century tower, a stair-turret, a nave roof featuring oversized saints standing on the unlikely foreparts of birds, florid bosses, and crude poppy-headed chancel stalls. Rustic carving on the pulpit panels shows a worm-like whale, Jonah's biblical monster. The adjoining hamlet of *Astrope* is buried in summer lanes of powdery cow-parsley by bright charlock-yellow fields.

Radlett [8] Wealthy 'residential area' spread out on either side of Roman Watling Street. Shopping thoroughfare is modelled on High Barnet or Golders Green. Of 'old Radlett' are the pretty flint cottages near the station and the church of 1864—coloured brick and flint among roadside trees. Tunnel up the adjoining Loom Lane to discover half-timbered gables set well back behind high-hedged frontages. Private roads ahead. In Gill's Hill Lane, near *Batler's Green*, in October 1823, lawyer William Weare was shot by boxer and gam-

bler John Thurtell, who had accompanied him by coach from London. Accomplices Probert and Hunt, a bankrupt and singing ex-coffee-house keeper respectively, helped stow the body in a pond, after which supper was taken at Probert's near-by cottage. The murder and the trial which followed the criminals' capture gained a powerful hold on the popular imagination. Thurtell's rhetoric impressed Hazlitt, and his execution was dwelt on by Lamb. Walter Scott prepared a scrapbook, J. D. Harding sketched the cottage, and the ballad-sellers made a fortune. Weare was buried in *Elstree* churchyard.

Radwell [2] Lane burrows under motorway, slides past church, a walled grange and a duck-filled lake and then peters out at a sign proclaiming (or demanding?) that 'Pig lorries stop here'. Pig farm ahead. Brick-patched and stucco-shedding All Saints' *church* has a Victorian timber porch and an exquisite little shingled spire on its bell-cote. Otherwise worth visiting for its Jacobean *monuments*. A miniaturized William Plomer (any relation of the poet?) prays in a niche next to his second wife Ann (d. 1625) and his heraldry and her whole memorial have been rudely repainted fair-ground fashion, predominantly in post-office red. Near by, Radwell's glory, Plomer's first wife (d. 1605) at 30—'Bewties flower/Cropt off in untymly

hower'—is modelled three-quarter-size in coldest alabaster. A zombie head shrinks into a cowl; dead fingers clutch an hourglass; and below, the eleventh and still-born child lies disregarded in swaddling clothes, a skull its pillow. Brothers and sisters are carved beneath. There are nice Tudor brasses and the Ten Commandments on the nave wall. Lakeside path from the church rubs against Bedfordshire county boundary and follows the *River Ivel* through woodland to Stotfold. Tarted-up *mill* commands lakeland views of birch and ash-trees flooded like mangroves.

Redbourne [5] Small town or large village? With a population of over 5,000 it outstrips Buntingford and yet its London-scale Georgian houses merely dignify, rather than transform, the thunderous *village* street. *The Common*, now a centre-piece with its cricket pitch, recreation ground and circlet of villas and bungalows, is really a larger, more exploited version of the rudimentary 'greens' so common to the area (e.g. at Cockernhoe, Chiltern Green, etc.). Leading off westwards from the Common, the cul-de-sac of *Church End* is composed of pretty brick cottages, an inn and a converted workhouse dated 1790, and seems a little picture-postcard village main street in itself. Completing the scene, St Mary's *church*, in its vast closed-in graveyard of part wilder-

Puttenham

ness, part Parks-Committee-style benches and paved paths, is a visual feast. It is basically a Norman building, having a sturdy tower and a north aisle arcade (similar to that of near-by Hemel Hempstead) of this period, that has been refurbished and enlarged particularly from the mid 14th to the very late 15th century. Chancel is recognizable as late Decorated by its flourish of chequer-boarding and ogee window tracery. Under the bricked embattlements of the south aisle and chapel runs an exquisite, moulded-brick corbel table, early Tudor, like that at Meesden (q.v.), which garnishes plain walling as a fringe does curtains or an ornamental border a Tudor title-page. Miraculous *rood screen* bears com-

parison with any of the famous Devon ones (e.g. at Lapford), with its intricate light caramel-coloured tracery and ribbed fan-vaulting stretched with a lacy skin of openwork. Dated 1478. *Monuments* in the chancel include a 1782 tablet of coloured marbles and a brass of 1560 to Richard Rede showing the family praying. By the M1, and half occupied by a modern sprawling 'hotel', are the remains of *The Aubreys*, an Iron Age hill fort similar to Ravensburgh Castle (*see* Hexton).

Reed [3] Statistically a remarkable village. Because of its strange plan of intersecting lanes it must hold the county record for the number of right-angled road corners for a

place of its size. Also, in a part of Hertfordshire noted for its moats, the concentration of six in a tiny area south of the main village is impressive. With a high point of 519 ft it is surely the county's highest village. On a clear day, it is said, Ely Cathedral may be seen from 'The Joint'—the wind-buffeted ridge route to Barkway. The cottages and houses and farms are arranged in a well-spaced entirely rural way in the lanes. There are no groups of buildings. At *Fiddlers Green* is the popular Cabinet pub. South of cricket pitch is a minute early Victorian schoolroom. Internally St Mary's *church* (mainly 14th century and restored) is disappointing. Outside, though, is a blocked Norman doorway and, rare in Hertfordshire, a trickle of Anglo-Saxon long and short work down the angles of the nave wall. In its moated grounds *Reed Hall* makes a pretty picture. The complete and partially wet moat, with mound, at *Gannock Green* is worth a walk to see. Overgrown and romantic. *Bush Wood's* moat has dark and scummy water. In the same wood wild cabbages grow like weeds.

Rickmansworth [7] Affectionately

known as Ricky. Although it never grew with the indecent haste of neighbouring Watford (with which it is nearly joined), Rickmansworth owes its spectacular rise from a sleepy, river-side backwater to an exclusive 'residential town' almost entirely to the arrival of the *Metropolitan Railway* in 1887. Expansion was slow at first: yellow-brick villas near the old centre, larger houses farther out, flashier shop-fronts in the High Street, a bit of mock timbering here and there. In 1901 a visitor wrote lyrically of the town's setting among water-meadows, of the scent of wallflowers everywhere, of the deer and titmice in the park to the north, and of the beeches of *Moor Park* to the south. A Griggs sketch shows women in bonnets and shawls strolling down dusty Church Street. Thirty years later the post-war Metroland mania had reached Rickmansworth. Lured by the prospect of living near this 'gateway to the Chilterns' town-weary City gents, unimpressed by Harrow and Pinner, were buying the £1,000 electric-lit gas-connected Tudorish houses being built in the grounds of ancient Moor Park, the best bit of which was now a golf-course. Simultaneously the town itself burgeoned, with Chorleywood and Croxley Green. Today it is expensive, but popular for the same reasons that made day-trippers up from London on the Underground visit and then settle. It is a town sliced up by rivers—the Chess, Colne and Gade—and canals—Grand Union and Grand

Junction. Tussocky water-meadows reach up to the churchyard wall and continue eastwards beneath pylon cables and railways towards industrial Watford. Weirs roar. The park, though smaller and seedier than in 1901 and dominated by the 'thirties *Royal Masonic School*, shoves a wedge of Chiltern scenery right into the town centre. There is woodland (albeit thin and motorway-slashed) between outer Rickmansworth and Chorleywood. The town centre is tiny and T-shaped. At river level there is a longish, rather narrow High Street, running parallel but keeping its distance from the much higher railway, which was originally built on the park edge. Between the railway and Metroland shops a cynical attempt at a car-park probably involved clearing buildings. Immediately east, facing old cottages, the new *Civic Centre*, although unpompous, inevitably jars. William Penn, founder of Pennsylvania, once lived at *Basing House* near by. The present building has a late 18th-century front. George Eliot lived farther east up the High Street at The Elms. The T's upstroke is made by Church Street—the only thoroughfare to keep its small country-town character intact. There are enticing glimpses of old Rickmansworth in the modest vernacular architecture and no chain stores, no Metroland. Tucked away in a courtyard, the *Old Vicarage* is sturdy late medieval with blatant additions from the age of the Picturesque. Corbels under the window are problematic. St Mary's *church*, big but lifeless, in a green churchyard of handsome Georgian headstones, has a tower of 1630, Regency yellow brick aisles, and the rest by Blomfield's dead hand (1890). Inside is a torrent of regulation pine pews, a brass, a table tomb, and some poor, framed plaster panels. Take the footpath from the churchyard to visit the *Bury* (Hertfordshire County Council) with its fine, old, panelled rooms. Church Street

swerves around the church to rejoin the late 20th century with a shuddering jolt and a roundabout.

Ridge [8] Extraordinarily long and

narrow parish, extending from Colney Heath to the Barnet bypass (before 1965 it reached to Arkley!) and taking in meadow, hills, deep woodland, and possibly, at its southernmost end, the unspoilt Hertfordshire countryside closest to London. This tiny, conventionally pretty village high up on its ridge has escaped any sort of development for some reason. *Church*, rather stark in its open graveyard by a scrappy green, has a slim, homespun 15th-century tower where flint, weathered stone and magical pudding-stone combine unassumingly. The plain interior is enlivened by a 15th-century wall painting of St Christopher, older stained glass and a crown-post roof. *Orchard Mead*, an almshouse-style affair by Sir George Gilbert Scott, has a delicious Kate Greenaway front garden. Near London Colney is the problematical *Tyttenhanger Park*, half-hidden by trees. The hipped roof, deep window pediments, and *brick* quoins imposed on the familiar Jacobean H-shape, fascinate and disturb. It is stylistically years ahead of its 1655–60 date and may be by the mysterious London architect Peter Mills.

Royston [3] Decidedly a frontier

market town torn between two worlds and two counties. Up at the south end by the bus station and market, one is unquestionably in Hertfordshire. There is timber-framing, much plaster, and some red Georgian brick upper storeys of shops; roads climb familiarly through chalk; expensive new estates invade beechwoods; and red villas overlook a neat *Festival of Britain* park. Down by the railway station, where the oil depot and massive white-brick flour mills stand at the brink of an endless plain, one could be in some light

Croxley Hall Farmhouse, Croxley Green, **Rickmansworth**

industrial Fenland town. There is early Victorian Cambridgeshire brick in Kneesworth Street, and in the back lanes tucked away between here and the Melbourne road, much recalls Cambridge suburbia, or even flinty Brandon. Until 1896, when it was diverted northwards, the county boundary ran down the middle of the present Baldock and Melbourne Streets, following the line of the ancient Icknield Way. Until Tudor times Royston was a handful of cottages and a priory by a dusty crossroads market place. The enigmatic *Roysia's stone*, preserved near its original crossroads site, gave its name to the town which only slowly grew up after the Dissolution and the founding of a 'palace' (really a glorified hunting-box) by James I. Bits of this affair, whose grounds took up a good half of Kneesworth Street's east side, can be picked out, notably a range with a striking shell-hood doorway. The most revealing views are from eerie, yew-hedged Dog Kennel Lane

slinking through woodlands eventually to join the grounds of Royston's premier early Georgian building, the stately *Manor House*, now a club. The royal kennels lie at the top of the lane, where some spooky ruins are glimpsed. Yet the town's most exciting relic predates everything but the stone. This is the *Royston Cave*. Unique in Great Britain, Europe, and possibly the world, the man-made, bottle-shaped chamber, the 'top' capped by a grille outside the National Westminster bank, significantly lies just east of the crossroads, its base being about 30 ft below the tarmac. Discovered by workmen in 1742 it was emptied of debris by treasure-seekers, who revealed its extraordinary chalk carvings. Dotty Dr Stukeley was notified. Theories (some crazy) have multiplied since. It is most likely that the crude images of martyrs, other saints, and religious symbols in a circular frieze are by the wily, bloodthirsty Knights Templar, who were active locally in late

Norman times. Present entry is along a steeply sloping tunnel cut in 1790. Before museumization by strip-lighting, railings and guide, casual visitors saw everything by candlelight—hence the blackened niches. Open on Saturdays; closed winter. St John the Baptist's *church*, though heavily restored, keeps its dissolved priory look, especially at the west entrance. Inside is much clever, probably 17th-century, reconstruction of original medieval work, and some genuine survivals: a pulpit made from the screen's Perpendicular tracery; 15th-century alabaster images and a rare knight effigy; 15th-century brasses; a pre-Reformation door and remains of stone bases left for 18th-century antiquarians. A scene filmily lit by plain, tinted and a spot of medieval glass. Hideous Victorian chancel. The graveyard of yews and handsome tombs melts into the town park. Don't miss Upper King Street, the best of which recalls faded water-colours and sepia photographs of town-

143

scapes that vanished with the horse and carriage. Shaded alleys, some green with elder, lead between decaying Georgian (and earlier) brick and plaster to racing stables that yield glimpses of the famous heath beyond. This is the frowzy, old country-town Royston of Rupert Brooke's black and fierce men—a world before the brewery closed and the industrial estate and overspill housing arrived. Experience it in a diluted form at the Wednesday auction (rabbits, cockerels, baskets of eggs), or in the funny colonnaded Corn Exchange of 1830 (Women's Institute marmalade, fishing tackle), or in the near-by coaching inns. Yet it is the rural Cambridgeshire which lives on, not hard pressed Hertfordshire. The Pasque flower and the celebrated Royston crow, after which the local newspaper is named, are heathland natives. In 1820 died Henry Andrews, 'Old Moore' of *Almanack* fame.

Rushden [2] A picture-postcard village. The tiny centre is off a through road from Cromer to Wallington on a lane that peters out past the hamlet of *Southern Green*—hence no traffic. Cottages of timber, weather-boarding, plaster, and flint are set in old-fashioned country gardens where golden rod is popular, and trim lawns are shaded by fruit trees. In Treacle Lane even council semis and private thatch (Risden and Flint cottages are idyllic) successfully commingle. On a hillock a *church* (St Mary) looks down upon, but is not separated from, the village by trees, It has a rendered flint nave and tower, and a cheery Victorian (1849) chancel of white brick which on the north side has attracted a bright Martian-green algae. The interior has a lived-in look with exposed electrics, bird droppings, G-plan pews, and a blue stair-carpet. A church of no one masterpiece but many modest felicities. Look up at the roof, at the 500-year-old beams, braces and

openwork spandrels, at the corbels supporting them. A seraphic lady, a grinning peasant, angels, a wicked leer, gaze down. Each panel of the octagonal font features six smaller panels of conventional 15th-century mouldings—a sort of pattern-book in stone. More mouldings of the same date decorate the niche in the chancel arch wall. A pity about the coy Virgin and child inside.

Sacombe [6] No village. Regency *Sacombe House* has ornamental parkland, and there are conifer plantations and wide views over bare hills from a black flint *church* of 1865 and its earlier stuccoed *Rectory*. St Catherine's is sullen and sombre, but contains monuments by Flaxman and Rysbrack, and a charming tablet to the Revd John Merton, rector here from 1637–69. At *Sacombe Green* the former Rectory is mullioned and jettied.

St Albans [8] Only 19 miles from Charing Cross is one of Europe's most striking cities. It has had a *cathedral* since 1877, when the abbey church was promoted, is a market town, and a residential and light industrial—but luckily not a tourist—centre. The cathedral cannot be escaped. Once belonging to England's premier abbey before the Dissolution, and with Europe's longest nave, it rears above the hill-top roofs, a mighty, almost talismanic symbol—built, like the vanished monastery, from the flint and red tiles of ruined Roman Verulamium across the river below. The medieval town was much smaller, far less ambitious in scale than, say, Hitchin, and lay under the abbey's wing, just to the north. Only with the Dissolution did housing ribbon away from the hub, along main routes—Holywell Hill, St Peter's Street, Fishpool Street—to create the skeleton of the present town. And yet today's centre of gravity is not the main shopping thoroughfare of St Peter's Street, but the cathedral and the streets around it.

Shabby façades in London Road, Victoria Street, and others appear alien impertinences, as do the chain stores, and indeed the *Civic Centre*. The prevailing character is strongly Georgian and early 19th century nevertheless, despite these intrusions. And some timber-framing has survived, a little of it on show, much behind plaster and brick fronts. Look for the essential St Albans between Romeland Hill and Verulam Road. Here, in and around Lower Dagnall Street, below the rubbed-out ramparts of Saxon *Kingsbury*, is a hilly quarter of brick artisan-type cottages, vaguely late Georgian, with here an *Independent chapel* of 1811 and 1846 *almshouses*, and there a bashed-about Presbyterian *Meeting House* of 1697; some inns; a glimpse of timber-framing down a side-street. In Welclose Street, in Verulam Road (built 1826), and in streets off it, stuccoed semis and terraces, some with huge frontages, recall Regency Cheltenham. Italianate *Christ Church* (1850) and *vicarage*, matched in honey-stone among trees, help the illusion. To the south, the cathedral always blocking the view; a stroll away to the west open countryside beckons. Winding down from the cathedral precincts to river level Fishpool Street is arguably the city's finest thoroughfare, perhaps the best in Hertfordshire. Most views are stopped by an almost interminable vista of cottages, town houses and inns of all periods from Tudor to mid Victorian, and of brick mainly, but featuring timber-framing, plastered overhangs, carved doorcases and some carriageways (it was a coaching route until 1824). South-side gardens slope to the river. Pokier north-side ones are formed from the Kingsbury ramparts. Some raised pavement, window-boxes, fresh paintwork, and smart urbanity. The biggest house is *St Michael's Manor*, which makes the whole thoroughfare—seen from Georgian weather-boarded *Kingsbury Mill* (pudding-stone in court-

Royston: (*left*) Courthouse; (*right*) former King's House

yard), with the *Black Lion* and *Blue Anchor* facing in the foreground—the simulacrum of a small-town main street in Essex or Suffolk. St Michael's Street likewise. St Michael's *church* stands where Verulamium stood until the 5th century and has Saxon flint walls incorporating Roman tiles. Later restorations are by Grimthorpe. Inside are a crude Norman aisle, Early English clerestory and lancets, a Perpendicular font, and brasses. Here is the seated effigy of Sir Francis Bacon of near-by Gorhambury: 'The wisest, brightest, meanest of mankind' (Pope). Having died from the after-effects of stuffing a chicken with ice, his body was brought here from London in 1626. All around in the water-meadows outside lie the excavated ruins of Roman Britain's chief city. Hunks of flint walling stand like strange sculptures. A crest of beechwoods plots the south-west boundary, shadowing the wall. From here drink in an unforgettable view of the cathedral and appreciate how the medieval town clung to the abbey's apronstrings. Walk along the *Causeway*, a broad ditch on one side, on the

Roman theatre, **St Albans**

other triple-layer sandwiches of flint and tile glowing palely. There is a superbly preserved theatre, a hypocaust (in a bungalow), and a museum containing the famous sea-god mosaic. Watling Street runs diagonally across the site and links St Michael's *church* with St Stephen's, another with Saxon work. Here is a Decorated arcade, but the ruling character is 15th century. The most rare eagle lectern is probably 15th century (Pevsner/ Oman). East of here, by river waste land, the brick, stone and flint ruins of *Sopwell Nunnery* gleam among ragwort and nightshade. However, what we see—smashed hood-mouldings, door lintels, 'bricks jig-sawed to the sky' (Peter Scupham: 'Sopwell')—belong to an Eliza-bethan mansion built on the site of, and using materials from, an early medieval Benedictine retreat. An intricate coinherence altogether. Banks of nettles, sprayed graffiti, and romantic ivy. Cottonmill Lane leads north to the old (i.e., pre-1796) London Road and an oddly shabby quarter of many inns. Sopwell Lane, narrow and featuring a line of timbered overhang and a medieval former inn, is a passable Tudor back-street. Holywell Hill has Georgian brick fronts that make it a gracious, unexpectedly

△ **St Albans** Cathedral

The Close, **St Albans** ▽

steep approach to the medieval centre. From it a path skirts the old monastery grounds to the river, to a mill which once polished diamonds, and to the well-known *Fighting Cocks Inn*. This queer, possibly monastic affair, has been a medieval pigeon-house, a dwelling-house, a cockfighting centre, then an inn, which it is now. A country lane climbs to the massive abbey gateway, now part of St Albans school, and into cloistered Romeland (once Roomland) and the cathedral-close atmosphere of Romeland Hill. Romeland House is magnificently Queen Anne. The *cathedral* provokes strong views. Or does it still? Lord Grimthorpe, a local landowner and lawyer with more money than taste, saw the great Norman church falling into a state of picturesque decay—plaster flaking, a weather-beaten west front, etc.—and sank much wealth into years of 'restorations' from *c*. 1878. Out went the old west front with its exquisite early Gothic porch; in came the deadly Grimthorpe version. Out went dull medieval windows; in came the 'banker's window', with its tracery in the form of coins of the realm. Lord Grimthorpe heightened aisle roofs, destroyed medieval ceiling escutcheons, swept away minor monuments, reset a brilliant Norman doorway and blank arcading quite absurdly into the south transept, and so on. Yet the deep monastic solemnity is undiminished, from porch to Lady chapel. Gimcrack confections, like Gibbs's reredos and the candle-wax chapel arcading, are betrayed beside the virtuosity of the Perpendicular stone rood screen, the stone panoply of medievalia guarding the *Duke of Gloucester's tomb* (d. 1447), the richer but less animated stone screenwork for the early Tudor *Ramryge chantry* (ogees, fan vaulting inside), and even the minutest figures of saints and ball-flower ornament around the early 14th-century Lady chapel windows. All around is Norman

power and oppression in the form of the church built in only eleven years (1077–88) by its abbot, lengthened and remodelled by a Gothic-minded successor, and improved thereafter by others. From under a threatening central tower a Norman arcade of massive shafts recedes into dimness and makes the later piers look spindly. Walls melt into gloom. Cotman-esque grace in the ochre-and-grey shaft decorations and in repeated motifs—chevrons, roses, diamonds, zigzags—inside the arches. North and south transepts, cosy refuges from the nave, have a triforium (i.e. gallery) sporting suspiciously Saxon balusters and probably looted by the Normans from an earlier church, which cleaves the unrelenting sternness with a rift of joy. Norman work ends at the presbytery, giving way to Gothic, that is to the lightness of rib-vaulting, of blank arcading, of fine Decorated tracery in the few windows. Chantry chapels and watching chamber close in on the *shrine of St Alban*. This miraculous reconstruction from 2,000 marble pieces of a crocketed, gemmed and gabled tomb-chest, shows carving that has been compared with that on the slightly earlier Eleanor crosses (*see* Waltham Cross). It was built *c*. 1302–8. Squeezed into a bay opposite, the timber *watching loft*, erected for monks guarding the shrine, has delicate tracery in its 'windows', juts out over fan-vaulting and a ground-floor of cup-boards and a staircase, and is carved with blank tracery and a frieze of rural cameos. It is *c*. 1400, quite entrancing, like every romantic's dream of some medieval craftsman's back-street cottage, and is very rare. Another *shrine*, this time of clunch and less successfully reassembled, is to St Amphibalus. There is much medieval wall painting apart from that on the nave piers—e.g. in transepts, nave clerestory, on a crossing arch—all familiar subjects and the remains of many that must have filled the

church. There is restored 15th-century work on the choir ceiling and Tudor roses in the tower. Unsurprisingly many brasses, mainly 15th century, and the Flemish example to Abbot de la Mare (d. 1396) is outstanding. But with ravishing stone screens around, brasses and tablets get ignored. The new chapter house, a stylish *tour de force* by William Whitfield & Partners, uses crimson Bovingdon bricks in an attempt to match the existing Roman 'tiles' in the main fabric. City's medieval quarter centred on French Row and the High Street is a picturesque jumble and a jagged roofline over which the plausibly ecclesiastical *clock tower* looms. This was built of flint *c*. 1402–11 and has five storeys and stairs to the top, where there is a curfew bell. The only other like it is at Morpeth. *Open to public*. Market Place is dominated by the *Town Hall* of 1829–31—rather over-sophisticated for its immediate surroundings and for the country Georgian character of St Peter's Street, which it heads. St Peter's *church* has an exterior dully restored by Grimthorpe and an interior which, apart from Perpendicular nave arcades, is deadlier still, and in a wholly Victorian way. *Monument* to the master-mason of Wren's St Paul's. In Hatfield Road are the ostentatious *almshouses* erected in 1736 by Sarah, Duchess of Marlborough. Humbler Jacobean *Pemberton almshouses* are tree-shaded and north of St Peter's. Catherine Street leads to Queen Anne *Dalton House*, nicknamed 'Bleak House' by those who thought it the Dickensian prototype, now engulfed in villadom. *Gorhambury* is a neo-classical mansion replacing Francis Bacon's Elizabethan seat, but retaining some of the famous gardens.

St Albans ▷
(right) The tower
(p. 150) North side of nave
(p. 151) North aisle

St Paul's Walden [5] Arcadian wooded landscape. Follow a lane which loops around the *church* to see all there is of this minute 'village'. From the outside All Saints', with its battlements, tracery, etc., seems a routine late Decorated and Perpendicular church. Only the round-headed chancel windows hint at what occurred inside *c.* 1727—a chancel 'repair'd and beautifi'd' in the English baroque taste by local squire Edward Gilbert. Barrel-vaulted ceiling and walls in moulded plaster with window surrounds and screen matched in general form and recently painted green with sugary carving picked out in white. Extraordinary how Hertfordshire's other remodelled chancels at Offley (1777) and Hexton (1807) lie in a straight line with this one. The decorative richness is echoed by gaily-painted Gothic Revival ceilings in an otherwise sober nave and chapel, and by the chapel screen's gilded tracery. Minor wall tablets include one that commemorates the present Queen Mother's baptism here in 1900. She grew up in the Bury. In the tower, and thoughtlessly obscured by a new organ, is a gorgeous early 14th-century Virgin and Child in mainly russet and green glass. The font is a bit sophisticated—very late Perpendicular with a frieze of leaves. In the churchyard there is an avenue of pollarded limes looking like multilimbed giants shaking their fists. The neo-Elizabethan and plain mid-Georgian *Bury* has gardens that are sometimes open to the public. Look out for the formal Georgian gardens, Gothick *garden house*, and other Picturesque paraphernalia.

Sandon [3] Long parish of ridges, chalk streams, scattered farms and lonely lanes. A village of council houses and cottages thrown together around the hump of a green and a pond. At the hamlet of *Roe Green* the cottages and chapel are set well back around a classic

St Albans: Under the tower (*above*); and in the south aisle (*below*)

◁ Humphrey, Duke of Gloucester's chantry, **St Albans**

153

English 'green', cricket pitch and ponds. The best Sandon group is the Georgian and earlier *Bury*, with outbuildings, viewed from the south-east with All Saints' *church* peeping up behind. The latter's flint tower is propped up by huge and incongruous brick buttresses. Inside the roomy, whitened nave are slim arcading and oak pews. Chancel, dated 1348, houses a show of eye-catching stonework; almost straight ogee arches, crocket-crammed for priests' seats; and finials and fleur-de-lis crowning a deep niche of the sepulchre opposite. There is a later oak screen of swaggering ogees and giant flower-heads and a Jacobean pulpit. *Monuments* of special poignancy to Elizabeth Moryson, d. 1626 in childbed, and Nicholas Miller, d. 1747, aged 18. The latter is a *tour de force* of tearful putti, leaves, fruit and flowers (symbols of blasted promise) wreathing a bust. Each September, at festival time, the church interior is flower-festooned.

Sandridge [5] Subtopian clutter in a village that has ribboned out to join St Albans. St Leonard's *church* seems outwardly unpromising until one spies Roman bricks in the chancel walls. Inside, a Norman chancel arch made of similar bricks is blocked up with an unexciting, but rather rare, Perpendicular stone screen. A bizarre sight. There are stylish late Norman arcades in nave and a pleasing Norman font of intersecting arches. Opposite the church, *Pound Farm*, mellow and ivy smothered, is guarded by four grotesquely truncated oaks.

Sarratt [7] Greatest asset is its green. Cratered by former ponds, girdled by detached or grouped half-timber and brick villas, its tussocked and hummocky length dips and rises for a third of a mile. A live duck-pond, an odd well and the cheerful Boot Inn add something.

◁ **St Paul's Walden**

On the corner (½ m. SW.) by Gothick-windowed *almshouses* of 1821 stands Holy Cross *church*, several times remarkable. Its size—it is tiny. Its shape—a cross plan. Materials used—flint plus a generous helping of magical pudding-stone for foundations; smaller hunks are used elsewhere; and Tudor bricks for gables and windows of the saddle-back tower, the only one in Hertfordshire. The interior has a dingy nave, short and cramped, with Norman arches, while the equal-length chancel has a sanctuary panelled and furnished like a miniature Edwardian drawing-room. Jacobean *monument* to William Kingley and wife is in agreeably faded colours, but for how long? Fragment of wall paint-

ing shows panoply of medievalia, including crowd, sheep and man playing ?shawm. At *Commonwood Common* is a rambling freak of a Victorian house. Other 'Englishman's castles' in the parish suggest that wooded, sequestered Sarratt, so accessible by Underground or main line, is a greater favourite with stockbrokers and bankers than Moor Park or Chorleywood. In 1852 Thomas Uwins, a water-colourist and Londoner, exulted in the Chess valley: '... Such woods, such meadows, such brooks!' he wrote home.

Sawbridgeworth [6] Small, mainly residential town. Malting is still carried on near the railway station and the River Stort, and

there are big old weather-boarded mills near by. The town is perched on a cliff above the valley and consists of four narrow streets intersecting near the church. Immediately to the west the old high road now acts as a sort of bypass, leaving the old centre virtually traffic-free. But who at the crossroads of The Square, Bell Street, Knight Street, and Church Street would imagine Sawbridgeworth to be the size (population some 8,000) it is? The buildings are of the familiar yellow-and-white brick with weather-boarding and plastering common—the former seen at its best in the overhanging upper storey of the old maltings(?) in Bell Street—plaster pargeting near by. But they are predominantly plain,

◁ *(left and above)*: Views in the grounds of The Bury, **St Paul's Walden**

157

two-storeyed, dormer-windowed *village* buildings, an Essex village maybe, a village which stopped growing here in the early 19th century but continued to develop along its high road (a *congregational church* of 1863). Only a couple of small red-brick Georgian houses in Knight Street, some large plastered houses of a similar date around the villagey Fair Green, and the handsome *Red House* in Bell Street, compare with the prosperous country-town character of say Hertford's Fore Street or Ware's High Street. And as a modern dormitory town it truly sleeps. Old-fashioned shops, a supermarket mimicking a village store, comfortable old inns like the *Bell*, with its Georgian bow windows, unchanged since Griggs drew it in 1901. The encircling suburbia is at a respectful distance and curtained off, thanks to trees and stopped views. *Church* of St Mary the Great, in a leafy churchyard surrounded by houses, is a swanky, dully restored Decorated building containing *monuments* that must be seen. Best is the opulent Jacobean wall monument to John Leventhorpe (d. 1625) and wife by Royal Mason William Cure. Burnished black and white marble. Fourteen kneeling children below—some females recessed to save space. Second best, though far more interesting, is a canopied sanctuary tomb smothered in crockets, ogees, panels of quatrefoils, and with brasses removed. Early Tudor. Mutilated figures on a near-by chest (of 1525). In an arch flanked by accoutrements of war—drums, pistols, daggers, sabres, trumpets, clutches of spears, all brilliantly realized—is the standing figure of soldierly Viscount Hewyt, d. 1689. Against chancel arch shiny busts set in grey bowls, of Jacobean period, are extraordinarily unconventional, recalling the portrait style of Peter Lely. The Viscount Jocelyn bust looks carved from plasticine or butter. Quality brasses include 15th-century nave types

and Tudor Leventhorpe examples in the tower. Brass of Beardsleyish lady, and pulpit of 1632. A vast oak chest with five locks. *Pishiobury*, to the south, and *Hyde Hall*, to the north, are Tudor houses remodelled respectively by James Wyatt in 1782, and nephew Jeffry Wyatville in 1803. Pishiobury is mildly Gothick, the more impressive Hyde Hall distinctly 'Soanian' (Pevsner) in its stuccoed details. The clan of farms with intriguing names like Crumps, Tharbies, Jeffs, Hoskins, are named after their medieval owners.

Shenley [8] Miraculously unspoilt country only 15 miles from Charing Cross. Mental hospital is larger than the village and incorporates the mansion of *Porter's Park*, once the home of Nicholas Hawksmoor, who is buried under a churchyard yew. St Botolph's *church* and a late 18th-century house lie together away from the village on the featureless road to St Albans. Both are empty and semi-derelict. After demolition of its tower and chancel the church, with its cellular flint blocks and brick dressings, now looks like a Gothic Revival chapel.

Sandridge: the chancel arch (*left*) and the font

boarding, plaster, plain and much grander Georgian brick, and grass verges, with a *church* (St Mary) a flint punctuation half-way along. Outside the village store stands a large pudding-stone hunk. Weather-boarded *water-mill* and *mill house* adjoin a Georgian-fronted medieval farmhouse at *Mill End*. Some remarkable features are preserved in the restored *church*. The original Early English chancel arch is lavishly carved and beneath it eight steps lead up to the chancel due to rising ground at this end. All the stained glass (poor too) is concentrated here, a dingy result, leaving the wide (widened by the Victorians) and lofty nave airy and well-lit. Elegant Decorated/Perpendicular arcades and an exceptionally interesting font, octagonal with shallow and chunkily-cut stylized leaves and tendrils. Allegedly 13th century, but so very Art Nouveauish. The 15th-century tomb monuments include delicately etched brasses on a chest to John F(i)eld and son. In the sanctuary are two high-class standing monuments to Sir Ralph and Sir Thomas Sadlier: effigies in niches, ribboning, obelisks, heraldry and cartouches figure. Both are Elizabethan in spirit. Outside is a detached tower, unique to Hertfordshire, and a roomy porch. Looking down from the lane following the ridge to *Barwick* ford, on to the river wriggling through newly-furrowed fields past lonely farmsteads, one instantly recalls the downland of Sussex or Kent. The far hills are of cinnamon silk, chalk stained; rough water-meadows and the *Lordship's* Tudor brick, with Standon's silver spire shining through leaves behind.

Stanstead Abbots [6] The smell of malt hangs over the terraced cottages and modern estate houses of this industrious Leaside community. In a staid High Street the high spots include: a cheerful grouping of the gabled *Red Lion* (with its jolly coaching-inn look)

Birds nest between window grilles and the Perpendicular tracery. The east window of imaginative modern glass brings welcoming gouts of colour. Tablets left on walls inside. A churchyard epitaph to a parish clerk and bricklayer, Joseph Rogers (d. 1828), claims 'none could excel/in laying bricks or singing well'. Eighteenth-century beehive-shaped lock-up in village. Fully-moated *Salisbury Hall* is of early Tudor and Restoration brick and contains very rare 15th-century clunch medallions from Sopwell Nunnery near St Albans. Near the moat and facing this city is a bricked-up entrance to a *tunnel* which is supposed to reach the Abbey 4 miles away.

South Mymms *see* Mymms, South

Standon [6] Huge hilly parish watered by the River Rib, which divides it. Roadside hamlets and scattered settlements, plantations, coppices, fords, and big farmhouses. Standon and Puckeridge are unidentical twin villages joined by the umbilical cord of suburban villa and estate housing. Standon's wide and mildly curving High Street is short and sweet, a low-key harmony of timber, weather-

picturesque in the extreme. Behind its shaded pondside drive the 16th-century *Bury* presents fronts of both William and Mary and Regency sophistication, which cannot fool the close observer, or the trained eye. The Perpendicular *church* has a brick chapel dated 1577 and an untouched timbered *porch* with crumbling flags that may have excited many an itinerant topographical water-colourist. Inside are cliffs of Georgian *box pews*, a three-decker pulpit, walls whitewashed to the roof-beams, and biblical texts everywhere. Demure tablets (and flashier ones) of the early 1800s and brasses. There is a churchyard view of misty Lea marsh lakes wrapped up in pylon wire.

Stanstead St Margaret's [6] Over the river from Stanstead Abbots is its unidentical twin, with villas by the New River, cottages towards Rye Park, the station and the disused *maltings*. From a distance the latter is easy to mistake for a late Victorian pile built for a banker. Nearer to, a skyline of cowls and chutes and a curious Italianate tower with spire are strangely haunting. *Church* (St Margaret's) lies in the green shade of yews, in an overgrown churchyard that overlooks the grounds of the timbered *Manor House*. Flint patched with roughcast and rendering, it has a Norman nave, and a Decorated chancel. The north aisle has been removed and the space blocked up with rubble. There is a tiny octagonal bell turret; box pews inside; and original tracery. Strikingly picturesque modesty.

Stapleford [5] Dull, Beane valley village on main road and railway. Alone among yews, with river-side walks from its graveyard, is the unfashionable, wholly delightful, *church* of St Mary. A stylishly individual remodelling job, dated

with the quirky *Clock House* of *c.* 1636 (mullions, quoins, weather-boarded bell turret); farther west the Georgian box of *Stanstead Hall*, playfully fortified with battlements and circular stair-turret; and, tucked away, Walford House also Georgian. All this is on an island formed by the river. Cappell Lane should be renamed after Alfred Waterhouse since it contains possible cottages by him (spot them!), his pedestrian St Andrews *church* (1880), and skirts the grounds of his monstrous red *Easneye* (1868–9). Better to gaze across water-meadows that recall Corot towards the chateau-like bulk of St Margaret's disused *maltings*. The Harlow road climbs from the valley, after the brick *Baeshe almshouses* are passed, then continues towards Stanstead Bury and *church* of St James. Both are

Sawbridgeworth (*above left and left*) the town; (*opposite*) Viscount Hewyt, by William Stanton, 1689

1874, on a Norman and late Perpendicular building has produced a timbered tower(with lead spire)-cum-porch which for pure form could not be bettered, and has left an eloquent Norman doorway of zigzags, and a meek, unspoilt interior boasting a crown-post roof. The outside walls are cased in cracked and flaking golden cement, tinted in places green and pink. There is a model Regency *rectory* up a sweeping drive.

Stevenage [5] The Georgian coaching town and modern New Town lie side by side in wooded country. Both should be visited. E. M. Forster's Stevenage, the town of his late-Victorian childhood and the 'Hilton' of *Howards End* (1910), has a broad and handsome High Street that has changed little since the novelist first knew it. Beginning unpromisingly with a grim Victorian brick chapel and an abrupt transition into the steel and concrete of the New Town, it blossoms out, slowly at first, with mid 19th-century cottages (now mostly shops) behind trees, into a wide and breezy country town thoroughfare, one of Hertfordshire's stateliest. Half-way along, the paved Middle Row (rather quaint) runs parallel to and then rejoins the High Street near some Georgian banks and the former *Old Castle* inn. In a barn here in 1724 the body of Henry Trigg, an eccentric grocer who spurned burial, was deposited in a coffin according to his last wish. A great 18th-century tourist attraction. There are more coaching inns: the *White Lion*, *Cromwell Hotel*, and the archetypal *Two Diamonds* and *Yorkshire Grey*, the last two adjoining. The Georgian *Grange* was the former *Swann Inn*, the town's most popular. In Stevenage's heyday, in *c.* 1800, over twenty coaches passed through every day on this Great North Road. The High Street fans out at last to encompass the triangular Bowling Green, around which are ranged a picturesque assortment of cottages. Opposite is the gable of the Tudor *Alleyn's School*—a jaded museum piece in its usurped school-yard. Budding out right and left (as Forster described them) from the High Street are the 'residential estates' which proliferated with the exodus from London to make 'old' Stevenage, with a population of around 6,000, a thriving town when the New Town plans were made. Today, despite new road-schemes funnelling traffic away, and the glint of new developments over the old rooftops, its original dignity and independence have survived. No ghetto of antique shops and delicatessens. One hopes Stony Stratford will survive Milton Keynes. St Nicholas's *church* was once aloof, but now peers down on the shining estates of *Pin Green*. It is important looking from the outside, with its battlements and herringbone-leaded spire on a stout Norman tower, but dullish within, or at least orthodox Perpendicular and Decorated and having bright early Victorian stained glass. There is good 15th-century carving on the screens and on misericords in the choir. A brass of a priest is *c.* 1500. On the Weston road, past

◁ **Stanstead Abbots** porch

Rook's Nest farmhouse, is the prototype for 'Howards End'. 'We had a very fine view . . . and to the north a peep of the park with its little woods of firs and oaks . . .', wrote Forster, recalling his childhood home. The novelist was furious when the *New Town*, a sponge for London's post-war overspill, came—the first buildings beginning to arrive around 1949 on the edge of the 'old' town. Thereafter a ring of farming hamlets—*Bedwell Plash*, *Chells*, *Broadwater*, *Pin Green*—and the whole village of *Shephall* were swept into the action to become bases for new 'neighbourhoods'. Each neighbourhood was given its own colour-coding on the Grand Plan, its individual 'neighbourhood centre' and sub-centre of shops, club and pub arranged in an intimate piazza fashion that has since become a hackneyed convention. Look for the streets named after eminent women, famous cricketers, explorers, poets, cathedrals, and trees. The housing is both council and private; detached and semi; short terraced and long; and dismal, exciting, and utilitarian in turns. Existing woodland has been requisitioned for communal use and open farmland turned into green spaces, many occupied by schools, which were designed to separate one neighbourhood from another. Of the bright new interlinking roads, some are in deep cuttings (e.g., near the church) some are drab dual-carriageways in the industrial area, and some are stretches snaking across the hilly wood and parkland of *Shephall* and *Broadwater*. At the development's very heart Whomerley and Monk's woods interpose a dark hornbeam world of real wildness between unmemorable urban *Bedwell*, above the town centre, and the more open, more rural, *Shephall*. In Whomerley the remains of a

Stanstead Abbots church ▷

medieval moated farmstead are part of a bird and wildlife sanctuary. Going eastwards Six Hills Way slashes through more woodland before it reaches *Chells* where a distant glimpse of thatch beyond a new roundabout is like a view into a Birket Foster. *Shephall* has snatches of imprisoned countryside around the green with its cottages, and near the small much-restored *church* of St Mary. This has a shingled spirelet on a timbered cage and inside, thanks to the removal of a ceiling, a roof of wormy medieval beams and trusses and modern rafters. The chancel arch is a curved truss, and the airy screen below looks contemporary, i.e., mid 14th century, but is possibly later. A bevy of comely Nodes *monuments* includes one to Jane (d. 1697). An extrovert nave window of tropical reds and yellows brings together peaches, marigolds and lilies. Gazing down from the heights of *Bedwell*, near modern semis that recall those of early Victorian Hackney, upon the cube forms of Stevenage town centre and the old orange roofs beyond, is like looking into an old town from its new suburb. The scale is friendly. A central pedestrianized shopping area of 1957–8 is encircled by later public and civic buildings, and though dated somewhat in its details, is far more welcoming than most later, brasher schemes (such as Birmingham's Bull Ring centre). Barrel-roofed St George's *church* narrowly avoids being mistaken for swimming-baths because of its pencil bell-tower. The museum beneath it is excellent. Even the tower blocks have dated, and 'brutalism', when it occurs, is of the provincial, inoffensive sort. Six Hills Way is named after the curious *burial mounds* by the old London road.

Stocking Pelham [3] Tiny, unremarkable spot on Essex border, with scattered farmsteads in narrow, twisting lanes, high-hedged in places. A cat's-cradle of an electricity station at *Crabbs Green* throws enormous wire hammocks across the horizon. A minute *church* on a sharp bend is simple, almost primitive, with its timber and slate bell-cot (replacing one struck by lightning in 1836), lime-washed interior, crude timbers and pine pews. There is a delectable Decorated, double-ogee nave window sitting askew and incorporating ropy medieval glass. A Pre-Raphaelite churchyard is shaded, overgrown, and overlooked by a big black barn. At *Rook's Farm*, in 1970, Mrs Muriel Mackay was held captive by the Hosein brothers and supposedly killed. Her body was never recovered.

Tewin [5] In wooded country and gracelessly expanded into a modern dormitory village. Alone in fields down a straight tarmac drive from the Georgian *Rectory* stands the *church*. Dottings of flint in a crumbly, honey rendering. An interior of cool tones, clean lines, and a certain visual fastidiousness which can irritate. Old stonework (including Norman window surrounds) is picked out from the lime-wash in the same spirit as fanatics expose beams. There are handsome cartouche tablets, a Georgian font, and clear glass of 1741 facing the blues and citric yellows of Patrick Reyntiens. Clanking Georgian clock. An international attraction is the churchyard tomb of Anne Grimston (d. 1713), who, it is said, declared that an after-life was as likely as a tree sprouting from her grave. She got her tree. A character in Forster's *Howards End* paid an astonished visit. Limb-like roots have smashed the tomb base and are lifting the tomb itself into the air, while the trunk consumes the original iron railings. *Queen Hoo Hall* is a story-book Elizabethan manor of burnished crimson and vermilion brick. *Tewin Water* has Repton-influenced grounds down to the Mimram and is early neo-Greek Regency.

Theobalds [9] Pronounced 'Tibbalds'. In 1590 versifier William Vallans gave us a flying swan's-eye view of Lord Burghley's 'new and worthie seate', begun twenty-six years earlier and since enlarged: 'The house it selfe doth shewe the owner's wit,/And may for bewtie, state, and everything,/Compared be with most within the land.' In 1607 Robert Cecil swapped it with James I for Hatfield Palace. The grounds were extended to encompass the wild hills and woodland westwards, and the whole surrounded by $9\frac{1}{2}$ miles of brick wall in 1620. Of this chunks remain at far-flung Wood Green farm. Of the grand house, demolished 1651, nothing remains but a wall fragment incorporated into a cottage in the grounds of *Old Palace House*—a seedily romantic spot between the railway embankment and leafy, litter-strewn Theobalds Lane. Facing a football ground (hence litter?) a good length of old garden wall is ivy-covered and has a tumbledown turret at the west end. Other wall chunks are in worse repair. The greatest attraction hereabouts is ($\frac{1}{2}$ m.W.) buried in the park proper where it was removed piece by piece in 1888 to serve as a gateway to the Georgian, half-hidden *Theobalds Park*. It is Wren's *Temple Bar*. Best approached, for those who like to be startled, along a muddy woodland track from the New River. Instant Baroque drama, with an Italian flavour. A grand central gateway for traffic is flanked by claustrophobic pedestrian tunnels; over the gateway is an upper storey with niches, pilasters, and a pediment decorated by cornucopias. Rain filtered through trees has washed city grime off all but the drapery folds on the battered statues by Bushnell and substituted, in places, a delicate green bloom. Stairway leads from a ruinous Victorian annex to an upper storey, roofless and crumbling. In all, despite graffiti, an image of magnificent, undefeated dignity. It needs selective restoration.

◁ Temple Bar at **Theobalds**

Therfield [3] Among trees the post office, inn, chapel and cottages gather around a tiny green with its 'best-kept village' sign, Near by, a short lane passes picturesque plaster and thatch on its way to the 'Old Rectory' (privately owned) and *church* of St Mary, rebuilt in 1878, incorporating original medieval fragments (corbels, font, tracery, and wooden angels) and an exceedingly rare cedarwood *monument* to Ann Turner (d. 1677). 'Old Rectory' is a delicious communion of mid 15th-century stone mullions, cusps and mouldings, and early Georgian red brick. There is a library of 1800, a 17th-century brewhouse, and, in the yard, a 270-ft well. Past rectors included the Duke of Wellington's brother and Henry Etough, an 18th-century eccentric who was possibly a vegetarian, teetotaller, and converted Jew. Footpath to Kelshall veers north to skirt some problematic moats and mounds that adjoin *Tuthill Manor*, an extraordinary sight. In a Herculean restoration effort by a teacher and his wife, a derelict, tiled and weather-boarded farmhouse became the present creeper-clad, timber-and-thatch 'dream home'. At *Chapel Green* (1½ m. S.) spectacular giant hogweed rules roadside and stream bank. *Therfield Heath* is the home of the rare Pasque flower and burnt-tip orchid—both jealously guarded. Adjoining the *Church Hill* beechwoods near by are little dells and hollows of yew and birch, scuffed-up chalk and blue flint chips.

Thorley [6] Chill landscape of wispy woodland, straggling hedges and enormous bare fields on the western edge of expanding Stortford. Drab ribbon development on A11, and (¾ m. W.) at the end of a muddy lane the medieval and Georgian *Thorley Hall* shares a romantic setting with the *church* of St James. This is flint clad in lime-washed cement, with only a spired tower and stonework left

untouched. Sculptured Norman doorway, ancient lancets, Victorian tracery, robust Georgian headstones and gloomy evergreens are sharp against the dazzling whiteness. Recalls the background to Hughes's Pre-Raphaelite *Home from the Sea*.

Throcking [3] A windy outpost high (147 ft) above the Rib valley has a water-tower, some bleak farms, and council houses in a sheltered lane. Off a bend in this lane, near a pond and some barns, elder-bushes and mud mark the site of the original Throcking Hall. To the north the present *Hall* is a bungalow. *Church* (Holy Trinity) has a plain Perpendicular undivided nave and chancel tacked on to a 13th-century, rather overbearing, tower with a hunched-up appearance. Lyrical brick stair-turret is contemporary with brick repairs to the tower (plaque dated 1660). A dull, unwelcoming, Victorianized interior is redeemed by dignified pews, poppy-headed stalls, and two *monuments* by Rysbrack and Nollekens—two of England's greatest sculptors. Tablet to Robert and Martha Elwes is by Rysbrack (1753). Hester Elwes (d. 1770) tablet, neo-Grecian, is by Nollekens and is masterly.

Thundridge [6] On steep hillside a *church* (St Mary) of 1853 by Ferrey replaced an abandoned building (½ m. E.). No evidence, however, that the medieval population shifted from the water-meadows to the present main-road site. No signs of a 'deserted village'. By the earthworks of an ancient Bury only a slender creeper-covered tower, mouldings smudged out by wind and rain, shoots up white against brambles and elder-bushes of an overgrown graveyard. It is tumbledown inside, with a cement-repaired roof, worn-off battlements, and graffiti. Perpendicular, it has a pointless Norman addition of a dog-toothed doorway. There are upturned and teetering

headstones among the yews. To the north a leaning chimney-stack once belonged to the vanished *Bury*, as did a crumbling brick wall. A footpath leads across a bridged island to *Fabdens*, a story-book medieval Wealdean house and a jewel, with its old doorways and old-fashioned garden. *Wadesmill* has plain Georgian cottages, three inns (two doubtless with a coaching past), and a road bridge with unusual 19th-century iron columns.

Totteridge [8] Absorbed into Greater London in 1965.

Tring [4] Popular commuter haven sitting under the Chilterns, but spreading its suburbia towards the Aylesbury plain. An eccentric little town with a unique name derived from the Anglo-Saxon 'Treung'. The main street is dull in a late Victorian sort of way but features at one end a bowery *Memorial Gardens* of benches and conifers and the famous *Rose and Crown Inn*. The architecture of giant carriageway and hopelessly sham timbers lurks in the mind and disturbs. Worth inspecting are the many alleys, courts and back-lanes around Akeman Street. A turn of the century observer saw in Willow Court, Tabernacle Yard and Denmark Place, shades of Shoreditch and Whitechapel. Today, even with a Chinese take-away a minute's distance, Denmark Place has an eerie flavour of Seven Dials or Edinburgh Old Town about it. Akeman Street itself is lined with humble artisans' cottages in the process of being gentrified. There are also some better Georgian and Regency houses and a chapel of 1832. In Western Road are some early Victorian terraces in orange brick and stucco which must have once been way out in the country. Completing the period scene the *Britannia Inn* has a well-preserved coaching air and must still delight travellers on the dull route from Aylesbury. *Church* (St Peter and St Paul), a Perpendicular and somewhat

Thundridge old church ▷

Walkern: Susannah Lewis monument

by the Rothschilds in 1873. Inside that casing of predictable 'banker architecture' is a putative Wren house trying to get out. Rothschild's *Zoological Museum*, now administered by the British Museum, houses a vast collection and is particularly strong in *Lepidoptera*. The rolling parkland gets pushed up into the Chilterns to memorable visual effect. At *New Mill* is a pretty 1818 *Baptist Chapel* tucked away by a stream, and a farm gate made entirely of agricultural implements. At some points along the dried-out track of the canal to Wendover can be seen original brickwork of the lock and drainage systems among nettles and hawthorns.

Walkern [5] Large, thriving, main-road village. The village street begins well with the chequer-brick *Manor Farm*, dovecot and pond, worsens with raw red brick, and finishes dominated by villas of the suburban sort. At this southern end there is some light industry. Near by, *Rook's Nest* is a dour citadel-like farmhouse. *Church of St Mary* lies past a ford by black barns and combines strong atmosphere and excitement with a sense of anti-climax. Saxo-Norman nave, with its elusive and problematical ?Saxon rood carving in chalk, timbered roof and screen, leads us to expect more of the chancel, which is all High silver-gilt gaudiness—a total let down. Early stone effigy of a 13th-century knight, his buckler clamped to his body, is only one of three in England with a visor covering the face. That inhuman head, carved coldly, speaks louder of its brutal century than the chancel's fancy piscina and sedilia. There are Victorian Op-Art windows of chevrons and squares, an index to brasses and Jacobean *monuments*. In the graveyard is an eccentric candelabrum monument of *c.* 1765. Across the adjoining field *Walkern Hall* looks the model country seat of a Regency banker.

restored chequered flint town church, stands alone and well back from the High Street behind a carpark where cottages once stood. (Notice the sad pear-trees of a ruined garden). It has a stodgy interior enlivened by amusing corbels that include: an antelope, a chained bear, a griffin devouring a knight, a fox and goose, and a monkey with a book and bottle. There is a pompous monument to William Gore (d. 1707), a Lord Mayor of London. Behind the church is a neo-Tudor *vicarage* in big grounds. *Tring Park*'s mansion was bought

Eleanor Cross, **Waltham Cross**

and atmosphere. A light-flooded nave, a murky chancel rebuilt in 1864 and nave pews of notched, gnarled and wormy oak, yet such delicacy, almost preciosity, in the fern forms of the chancel arch capitals. Shades of Southwell Minster! The north chapel stained glass, reddish oak screen and table tomb with frieze of saints in niches, are all 15th century. At *Redhill* hamlet ($\frac{1}{2}$ m. SE.) is the site of one of Hertfordshire's oldest Nonconformist *chapels*—built *c.* 1720, rebuilt 1805. Only a damp, bramble-infested graveyard by a brick shed remains.

Waltham Cross [9] Urban southern appendage of Cheshunt named after the famous *Eleanor Cross* which once dominated a busy crossroads. Today that monument, one of twelve erected by Edward I along the route taken by his wife's funeral cortège, competes for attention with the brashest of red-brick shopping complexes and an ill-placed old inn sign of four carved swans. Work on the cross was begun *c.* 1291 and soon finished. Materials used included Caen stone, Sussex and Purbeck marble, and precious stones – total cost, £95. The present railed-off 40-ft affair is the result of rain and frost and unsympathetic 19th-century restoration—the original statues are now in Cheshunt public library and, indeed, the cross narrowly escaped being re-erected with Temple Bar in Theobalds Park. In style the carving heralds a departure from the simple flowing lines of the early Gothic towards the busier, more sophisticated Decorated manner, with its florid curves, crockets and finials.

On the Cheshunt road No. 256, a former wayside cottage with weather-boarding, holds its own against an office block. In 1859 Anthony Trollope came to live in Waltham Cross as head of the General Post Office's eastern district. He grew strawberries, roses and cabbages, kept pigs, and wrote five of his best novels here.

Wallington [2] George Orwell's village. With his wife (whom he married here) he kept the general store from 1936 until 1940. He paid 7s. 6d rent, raised hens, grew potatoes, wrote *The Road to Wigan Pier*, and many book reviews and essays here. Village pub (matchbox collection inside), cottages and a school make up a street which slopes down to a muddy field. *Church*, huge *Rectory* and *Bury* lie together on higher ground to the south. *Church* (St Mary), wholly Perpendicular, is an affair of contrasts—grand, yet with intimacy

Ware [6] Small residential, light industrial and malting town on the River Lea. Always Hertford's rival, and for centuries its more prosperous neighbour, Ware is only just (1980) beginning to shed a shabbiness brought about through a combination of planning blight, civic apathy, and general feelings of inferiority. A huge trade in corn and malt made 18th-century Ware wealthy and gave its centre a characteristic country-town Georgian appearance. Grain barges would return from London along the Lea or the New River with cargoes of coal. Further business came from coaches using the Great Cambridge Road through the town. Hertford had no such advantage. Yellow-brick Victorian Ware grew apace, especially along New Road and up Musley Hill, where early railway commuters, or the retired, evidently favoured views over the Lea Valley. But the 20th century brought Hertford a grand county town role, and a civic centre, and Ware much overspill housing and a College of Education, but little to compensate it for the loss of its status as 'the largest malting town in England'. Approach it from London Road where an old *maltings*, Georgian cottages and the former home of the Quaker poet Scott overlook New River, the railway (period gem of a hotel opposite the station) and flour mills towering over the Leaside wharves, where, at the bottom of some High Street gardens, timbered *gazebos* are reflected in the water. Amwell End and Bridgefoot, both spoilt by neglected property and shopping parades, symbolize the blight. The modern *Saracen's Head*, totally out of character, replaces the Georgian home of the famous 'great bed of Ware', now in the Victoria and Albert. Also sadly demolished was a range of huge barns used as corn stores in near-by Star Street, and maltings at the

◁ **Ware**: the Lea east of the bridge (*above*)

Pumping Station on the New River

The Lea west of ▷
the bridge

town's northern end. Yet somehow the longish High Street has survived intact. It is strongly Georgian in mainly red brick, with old inn carriageways, a few original shopfronts, a bit of plastering here, some timber-framing there, interrupted half-way by a market place too small to be functional, and closely tracked its whole length by the glorified alleys that are East and West Streets. In the former, look for the carriageway (with niches over) let into some dowdy Queen Anne fronts that screen the *Bluecoat Yard*'s late 17th-century, almshouse-style brick cottages from the workaday bustle. The recently 'face-lifted' *Place House* opposite began as a

14th-century manor-house and became the Bluecoat School from 1674–1761. West Street is hardly recognizable as the picture-book affair of plastered gables and ovehangs drawn by F. L. Griggs in 1900. Farther behind the High Street, Church and Cribb Streets are homely small-town back-lanes of red and yellow cottage brick and harmonious black weatherboarding. The town's auction rooms in Church Street were once a 1778 Independent chapel preached in by the political philosopher William 'Caleb Williams' Godwin, when a minister. The High Street curves and then opens out pleasantly to accommodate a big

flint *church*, well back in its formal graveyard, and facing, down by the river, the white stuccoed *Priory*, whose original 15th-century windows are well hidden on the south side. There is a delectable view of Baldock Street's ancient roof-tops from the churchyard, which incidentally contains Ware's best modern development. By the roundabout which ruins Baldock Street is the *Bull's Head*, a coaching inn of character. Inside, a wooden 6-ft list records all the town's inns, past and present. St Mary's *church*, an over-restored mainly Perpendicular affair of Decorated origin, is unexciting despite its size and pretensions. There is some original

(left and above) Burne-Jones stained glass at **Waterford**

The Grove, **Watford**

stonework, including a high Perpendicular font carved brilliantly with saints in niches and angels bearing harps. Some individual Victorian stained glass; some Byzantine exoticism in the chancel; and an Elizabethan effigy looking like ripe Gorgonzola. Unusually, the transepts have clerestories. There is a romantic walk with good valley views from Park Road through to the grounds of *Ware Park*, a Victorian ex-sanatorium which was built to replace the home of Richard Fanshawe (1608–66), Royalist toady and 'poet'. Another

local writer, the Quaker John Scott of Amwell, deserves more attention. Born in Bermondsey in 1730, he came with his father to *Amwell House* (now part of Ware College) at ten and, with the eventual inheritance, began transforming his grounds into a private, highly artificial, almost paradisal world. In his acres of verse, collected and illustrated with plates engraved by the young William Blake in 1782, Parnassian dross far outweighs the sharply focused imagery. And yet *Amwell* (1776) is worth reading for the occasional cinematic passages

that proclaim a landscapist's vision: '. . . delicious hills/Bounding smooth vales, smooth vales by winding streams/Divided, that here glide thro' grassy banks/In open sun, there wander under shade/Of aspen tall, or ancient elm, whose boughs/O'erhang grey castles, and romantic farms . . ./from Raydon's pleasant groves/And Hunsdon's bowers on Stort's irriguous marge/By Rhye's old walls, to Hodsdon's airy street;/From Haly's woodland to the flowery meads/Of willow-shaded Stansted . . .' Not surpris-

174

ingly Scott wrote eclogues, and also political pamphlets, volumes on highways and turnpikes, and some literary criticism. His garden *grotto* took eighteen years to build, cost nearly £10,000, and used local flint as a background for a sequin show of quartz, broken coloured glass, and pebbles. A friend brought back giant conches from the South Seas. And it survived, albeit neglected and vandalized! A Gothick *gazebo* on a knoll peeps above modern gardens. Labyrinthine tunnels with rooms off at intervals, all decorated, can be explored by torchlight. An inexplicably sad monument, even in its romantic decay.

Wareside [6] Ordinary streamside place in attractive country above the River Ash. The yellowish-brick Holy Trinity *church* of 1841 is vaguely neo-Norman despite its interior galleries. In the garden of the house opposite Babb's Green phone-box are overgrown tracks, a brightly-coloured station and a locomotive of the *Emerald City Railway*.

Waterford [5] Roadside cottages and pines at the point where the valley of the River Beane mimics the Wye Valley. A narrow lane corkscrews down from the railway and sand workings, past hawthorn scrub to meadows, a stuccoed house and the modest brick bridge. Hillside *church* (St Michael) is appropriately of ragstone and has a bold, timber-shingled spirelet and a generous porch. It dates from 1872. The inside glows with probably the best show of 'William Morris & Co.' glass in the county. There is work by Morris himself, Burne-Jones (some brilliant designs), Ford Madox Brown, and Philip Webb—scintillating.

Watford [8] Contrary to popular belief Watford is not in London; but to many travelling on a southbound express the metropolis appears to start somewhere between here and Hemel Hempstead. As the train curves out of the

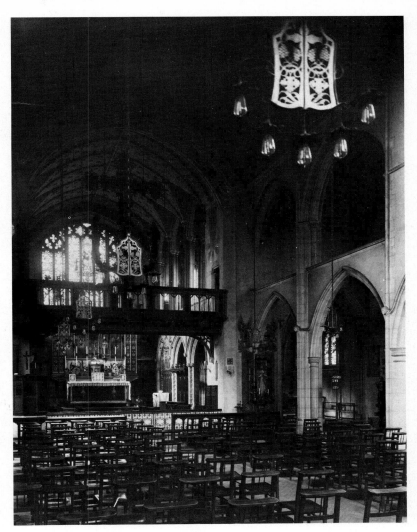

J. F. Bentley's Holy Rood church, **Watford**

junction, high on its viaduct, there, spread below, are the gasholders and waste-sites, the hoardings and the rows of shabby stock-brick terraces of some far-flung residential suburb. On the pavements of North Watford one could be in East Ham or Tooting. There are even five Underground stations. To appreciate fully Watford's separate identity, and its strong status as the largest town (77,000 people) in Hertfordshire, one must be prepared to explore without prejudice. Beneath the viaduct and road bridge the Colne wriggles north-

wards in a semi-rural setting towards the open country at Bricket Wood. *Cassiobury Park*, to the west, touches the town centre's A412 at its most brutal point—just as it imitates the Euston Road underpass. Thus, from road schemes, from the monolithic neo-Georgian Town Hall, and from the banalities of the remodelled shopping quarter, one may escape into walnut and oak groves that lead eventually into Chiltern woodlands—and still be in Watford! The River Gade/canal walk takes one through wooded meadow to

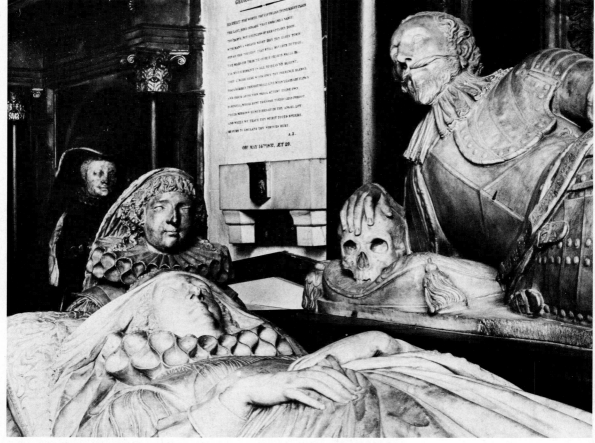

(*above and opposite*) Morison monuments at **Watford** by Nicholas Stone

Grove Mill, a jaunty conversion of a yellow-brick Victorian building that has a foaming mill-race, and from here to *The Grove*, a Georgian mansion, with an unfortunate corrugated iron roof, set on a hill. In pasture below a delightful balustraded canal bridge of *c.* 1800 is stupendously white against the bright grass. And Watford's housing estates are only a screen of trees away. The A4145 to Rickmansworth threads its way through scrubby meadows where horses graze in mist among the tangle of river, railway and pylon. Surprises abound. The town is long, but slim-waisted and rather top-heavy with acres of housing pressing down on the essentially small historic core of church, market place

and lengthy, spinal High Street climbing up from the river. Until very recently Watford had one of the best collections of timber-framed buildings in the county in its High Street. Alas, thoughtless demolition has taken its toll. Of Benskin's magnificent *brewery*, the town's pride, only the plain Georgian offices have survived (now a *museum*)—and new developments are now filling the gaps. The street closes on a low note, with giant hoardings and a gasholder blocking the view ahead and a battered Georgian *Frogmore House*, rather handsome, looking ill at ease. Parish *church* of St Mary—Perpendicular, in dully restored flint and off an alley in the High Street—is worth visiting for its 1597 *Morison*

chapel and *monuments*. These include a Charles Morison effigy (with wife) of *c.* 1628 in which the couple lie in an enormous black marble four-poster affair—'splendissimo' indeed. There is another of similar design and date that features a bold, red-veined marble, and, in another, Dorothy Morison (d. 1618) is modelled kneeling. There are also some good 15th-century brasses and baroque cartouches. A brownness of stained Victorian oak and burnt toffee roof-timbers is all pervasive. In the dingy graveyard the tomb of Ben Wangford sprouts a fig-tree. The long, bright yellow-plastered *Bedford almshouses*, richly picturesque, shut off one side of the churchyard; Elizabeth Fuller's *Free School*, a rare